You, Me and Them

You, Me and Them

by Elijah Levy, Ph.D.

iUniverse, Inc.
New York Lincoln Shanghai

You, Me and Them

iUniverse, Inc.

For information address:
iUniverse, Inc.
2021 Pine Lake Road, Suite 100
Lincoln, NE 68512
www.iuniverse.com

ISBN: 0-595-31361-2

Printed in the United States of America

A book about cultural diversity, tolerance, and ways to think about people from other cultures. It's all very important because sometimes it's hard interacting with people who look and talk differently. I mean, we're all unique. Without diversity it would be boring around here. Remember now, you can only eat so many of the same plain brown M&Ms. Know what I mean?

To Dad, master storyteller of an adventurous and righteous life and Mom, who taught me how to live a virtuous life.

Contents

Acknowledgments

All right. I need to acknowledge individuals that have supported and tolerated me while writing this book. Yes, tolerated me because I can be irritating, but just a little bit and only with certain people. I've spent three years on the launch pad writing this book. It's okay sitting on the launch pad for three years as long as you know where the launch button is, know your launch destination and can estimate how long it'll take to launch. The fuel doesn't necessarily go bad after three years, and the technology doesn't change too much. So, now you know how long it's taken to launch. How do you like this metaphor of launching for achieving goals?

I suppose you're interested in knowing why I wrote this book. It's because I'm interested in easing racial and cultural tension and increasing cultural harmony. I like educating people about other cultures and their culture bound values. We all need to generate awareness by identifying our cultural assumptions and counterproductive biases. Interestingly my students discover that their biases and stereotypes are unsubstantiated when checked against reality. The last reason I wrote this book is because my wife insisted I establish job stability as a writer, which translates to generating revenue as a writer. Know what I mean?

I need to thank all of my courageous students enduring Schizophrenia, who taught me they aren't the "otherness" humanity labeled them as representing. You are valued human beings first, terribly misunderstood second, and unfairly stigmatized third. You defeat social forces that distance you from us, label you socially marginal, yet strive to live a meaningful and purpose driven life. I admire each of you for refusing to surrender to your illness and allowing it to consume your total identity and life. Thankfully, we've got each other. We partner real well and teach each other so much. You know that learning empowers you to be self-determined. You control your life and the conditions that affect your life. We're great partners in life.

I need to acknowledge my real good friend Purandar Mallya, M.D. Purandar, your life work treating the mentally ill is extraordinary—there's no other psychiatrist like you; totally dedicated to reaching our consumers through your empathic voice and touch which looks beyond psychosis to validate that significant human being. Your friendship means so much to me. Purandar, thanks for the reminders to finish the project.

I know, I haven't forgotten about my older adult students at Norwalk Senior Center and La Mirada Activity Center. I'll admit, all of you have enriched my life tremendously. There's something special about each of your unique personalities, and well, you know how I feel about you. I pretty much like all of you. I admire your pursuit of lifelong learning and passion for living full, engaged and meaningful lives. You know, we've got a fancy way of saying it: creative aging. All of you know what to do with the fastballs and curves headed your way, and you've coached me pretty well. Although I'm the teacher, just between you and me, you've taught me lots more than I've taught you. So, together we launch big time. Remember now, all of you mean a lot to me. I mean it now.

I'd get into serious trouble if I forgot to mention my little brother Joe and his wife Lysa. All right, I mentioned them. We're done. So, in addition to being a Lieutenant with the Long Beach Police Department, my brother teaches cultural diversity and human relations to peace officers throughout the country. Joe doesn't know as much as me though, and I'm the one with the Ph.D. Lysa who is the Program Director for the National Conference for Community and Justice in Long Beach, is equally committed to teaching tolerance, and workshops on human relations and leadership skills. Joe and Lysa, you're great teachers.

Now, my parents. Nessim and Esther, both of whom were born in Egypt, and moved to Israel as young adults, inculcated in me a bias-free attitude as a child. My parents modeled empathy first, followed by teaching how to do for others. Dad, thanks for engendering the expression of my curiosity instinct—I learned it from you; that learning other life ways added depth to my life. The only problem I encountered was I didn't speak seven languages as fluently as you. Naturally, it made it easier for you to understand other cultures. Mom, your unconditional social caring for others is unbelievable. You taught me to extend my hand to the less able. My parents taught me early on that our G-d was a deity of action—and that we were commanded to perform acts of kindness, obey moral codes to do the right thing and when possible, prevent social injustice. The Jew's obligation to repair the world is termed "Tikkun Olam." Unconditional social caring was an absolute. Nessim and Esther, I can't sum up your incredible, enduring influence on me in a paragraph. What I can do to preserve your legacy is continue teaching empathy, doing the right thing, tolerance, unconditional acceptance and the virtue of social caring to our children.

Now, my wife Nora and my daughters, Elise and Diane. Nora is a gift of everlasting love; she gives and gives; in her support and understanding. She is my indispensable partner. Nora read and offered suggestions on the manuscript. Actually, she's used to giving me advice on lots of things. She understands and experiences tolerance because she lives with me. I'm sorry I was consumed with writing this book. Nora, saying thanks isn't enough, so I'll get you something nice and not on sale. Elise and Diane, thanks for providing me with opportunities to practice open-mindedness. You are both thoughtful, well meaning children who understand the importance of showing positive regard for others. Elise and Diane, thanks for your comments on the manuscript.

Elijah Levy, 2004

1

Enrichment: Hey, I Don't Need Enriching. You're Confusing Me With That Guy Over There Who Needs It

o o o o o o o o o o o o o o o o o o o o o o o o o o o o o o

"Men are wise in proportion, not to their experience, but to their capacity for experience.

—*George Bernard Shaw*

"He who adds not to his learning diminishes it"

—*The Talmud*

Thanks for purchasing this book and showing an interest in this subject. Of all the things you could be interested in reading or spending your money on, you chose cultural diversity. Admit it now, you're pretty much interested in learning about diversity. Isn't that a fascinating subject? Discovering the different ways people live and everything that's related to living, like creating a culture of shared meaning through language, cultural artifacts, myths, and religion. Do you want to really be fascinated? There are no anvils, bulldozers, fancy cell phones, topical ointments for severe and persistent itches, or computers in lots of cultures that sustain themselves. Oh yeah, the people in these cultures also feel important, worthwhile, secure and they have

1

positive self-evaluations of themselves. In other words, they have good self-esteem. See, I told you cultural variation is incredibly interesting.

Why didn't you pick up a magazine about the National Hot Rod Association? Or even better, a book on neuropsychology to learn about the relationship between chemical substances and behavior. I'm talking about chemical substances that are naturally in your brain, such as serotonin and dopamine, and their relationship to your behavior. It's pretty much about the brain-behavior connection. Reading about neuropsychology would clearly enrich your life. With the hot rod and drag racing business, you'd get a major introduction to a fascinating subculture of incredibly fast top fuel cars, funny cars and pro stock. I'm not sure, but it may also be about country music. I once knew a neuropsychologist who was into hot rods, country music and Thai food. I mean, there's nothing wrong with it. He liked eating a lot of that Thai barbeque chicken.

Are you required to read this book for a class? Listen, I've got nothing to do with it. I don't even know your teacher. I just wrote this book and had nothing to do with requiring you to read it for your class. I'll be honest though. I teach, and because I need the money, I may have required you to purchase this book for one of my classes like Introduction to Sociology or Multicultural Issues in the Community. If you're one of my students, I'm sorry about this lousy situation you're in. Don't feel powerless. Look, there are lots of worse situations. This could have been a book on entomology and entomostracans, you know, small crustaceans. Or I could have assigned another book like Sartre's *Being and Nothingness*. This book is simply about human beings being aware of themselves, of having to be responsible for themselves. Being responsible for yourself means admitting you and only you are willfully directing the outcome of your life. It's pretty much about you exercising your free will. Others may influence your thinking and feelings, but in the end, it's pretty much you making decisions that hold you responsible for what happens to you 24 hours a day, seven days a week, 42 weeks a year.

Human beings are responsible for themselves. What an incredibly incendiary statement. Incendiary means willfully stirring up problems. It's typically used to describe someone causing a fire, rebellion or riot. I looked it up in the dictionary. In the context I'm using it in, it refers to someone causing somebody else to get angry. Know what I mean? We're talking about human beings acting in responsible ways. Now can you see why asking human beings to be responsible for their behavior has a great potential to be incendiary? It's a potentially incendiary subject because human beings who make poor choices don't like admitting they did. Although they willfully and consciously made the choice to act a certain way, they believe someone else or a mysterious social force made them do it. All I know is there's lots of mysterious social forces' out there making people do things they don't want to do. Maybe it was their alter ego. Everyone's got an alter ego; an intimate, usually agreeable, life-long companion who lives with you, and is always watching you and talking to you. Did you know you actually control how your alter ego feels about you? Remember now, your alter ego can't control how you think and feel about things, neither can a mysterious social force control your alter ego or how you think and feel about things. *You* control your alter ego and any mysterious social forces out there trying to get you to make lousy choices or misbehave.

Now, I'm not going to reveal anything insightful here, but some people avoid assuming responsibility for their poor choices and the unfavorable outcome of their behavior. That's pretty much it on this thing. In the final analysis, no one asks me where he or she can go to get into trouble. The courthouse, bail guy and police department are down that way and I always walk the other way, as far away from these institutions as possible. Know what I mean? I've never allowed a mysterious, powerful social force to lead me to the police department, bail bond guy or the courthouse. I've also never let my alter ego get me into trouble and land me in jail. My alter ego pretty much gets along with me.

Did you notice that I wrote 42 weeks a year instead of 52 weeks a year three paragraphs ago? If you did, then you passed your first "Yes, Captain I'm awake" check. If you didn't then you're probably experiencing attention and concentration difficulties at this time. "At this time" pretty much means right now. Consider this first alertness check a practice one, and look for more of them. Listen, don't get angry with me. I'm just trying to keep you awake. Too bad you can't give me an alertness check. I'd pass it for sure. I'm always paying attention and concentrating on things. It's just too bad there's no way for you to give me a "Yes, Captain, I'm awake" check. And yes, I pass the alertness checks other people give me.

If you're an ordinary, conforming person you'll become culturally diverse and still retain your ordinary, conforming traits when you finish this book. Your personality traits are pretty enduring and color how you view the world, so reading this book probably won't change your personality traits. Reading this book is an educational experience; you'll become lots more culturally enriched when you're done interpreting and reflecting on important things and softening yourself up for an awakening. It's sort of like an integrative experience. In other words, it will all come together after you read the last word. Don't jump ahead to the last page now, because it won't help. There is a beginning, middle and end to this journey we're on. You've got to read this book to genuinely achieve a raising of your consciousness. If you don't, it's like cheating and pretending you got something out of it. You'll have a fake enrichment experience if you skip to the last page. Who wants to have a fake, inauthentic enrichment moment? *Do the work and read the book, cause if you don't, you'll miss the look.* You know, the "I got it" look. Now you know why I'm not a poet. Although that wasn't so bad. Was it? And no, you wouldn't rather be reading that hot rod magazine. Remember, I need the money and you need this indispensable book. It's not necessarily in that order.

Thanks for Buying the Boo

Look, $13.00 may seem like a lot, but remember I'm paying too and well, I'm not making as much as you think I am on it. I'll make a lousy profit for sure. So, don't be thinking, or have this illusion I'm in my Mercedes. I'm actually in my 1987 Volkswagen. It's a Westphalia, you know, the pop-top camper van. It's the Wolfsburg Edition, which means it's a high-end camper van. You'll know it's the Wolfsburg Edition because it's got the very nice Wolfsburg decal on both sides near the driver and passenger door. I love my van. It's an expensive piece of machinery. It has 90 horsepower. I'm not into power and speed. It's also got an AM/FM C.D player and a very nice, small refrigerator.

Anyway, I know we're going to get along fine. Just drop the $13.00 aggravation and stop thinking about it. Think about other things. Thirteen bucks is what it might cost you for lunch or something, especially if you've got a friend at work that you treated to a sandwich. Don't you have friends at work? Inform them about this great book. Just think about which friends you could talk to about my book. No. You know what, do something totally ridiculous like think about how the book will enrich your life. Now, wouldn't that be something? If you did you'd be more likely to keep the book and say favorable things about it. I'd like that for sure. I'd really like you to buy another book. I mean, you can give it as a gift or something. Can we talk about it later?

All right, So What is Diversity?

Diversity means differences. My goal is to get you to understand that understanding differences means accepting the understanding that it's okay to be different and still understand each other. You understand? I mean, that's the definition of diversity. I think you got it. Writing for me is a sort of social and personal activity. I'm writing now because I've got something to say, someone to say it to, (which is you) and there's a clear purpose for why I'm engaging you in this process.

Now, you'll understand what I'm explaining, because I always articulate myself nicely, with great clarity and prose that effectively conveys my message. That's why I'm always easily understood. And yes, I know I used the word understanding four times in that first sentence in the previous paragraph. I really don't need you to point grammatical things out to me. It's another "Yes Captain, I'm awake" check. Most people who know anything about the English language would have picked this up. You know, about not being allowed to use the same word four times in one sentence. All right, so did you pick it up? Be honest now. No one else is going to know except you and your alter ego.

If you haven't noticed this yet, you will now. I develop and communicate my ideas nicely because I have a very good grasp of the mechanics of writing. I actually have a very good grasp of a lot of things, but right now we're discussing writing. My sentence structure and language usage is also very well developed. I have great critical thinking skills, and am insightful, which allows me to write in a way that demonstrates an in-depth analysis of things that are complex. You've probably noticed this by now. Also, I can illustrate key concepts we're discussing with very good examples. I mean, the examples are pretty good to me.

So, are you accepting, tolerant, respectful and compassionate or irritating? I sure hope you aren't inflexible, overly self-indulgent, arrogant, resistant, overly critical, or needing to be right all the time. How are you with boundaries? You know, about listening to that soft voice in your head that advises you to STOP NOW. Listen, there are too many people saying, "I know I'm right about that thing" and they're probably right about lots of things in the world. I sure hope you're not one of those people. Are you?

The Endless Need to be Right

Let me ask you something. Have you ever let some poor, needing-to-be-right, unassuming soul be right out of your unselfish desire to truly want to indulge the poor fella? Out of your compassion for the person, you invest yourself in getting this poor individual to feel better about him or herself because this person has a whole lot of problems? I guess it would depend on what you'd let them be right about. And no, I'm not letting you be right because you're the poor, unassuming soul who needs to be right to feel better about yourself.

Establishing the Author's Legitimacy

I wrote this book. I know some things and I'm not that poor, needing-to-be-right, unassuming soul. Yes, I've got about one vulnerability but it's too soon to be discussing it with you now. I should inform you that I have a Ph.D. That's not the vulnerability. You know, a doctorate degree. And yes, I'm fully aware that my Ph.D. may represent the equivalent value of a lousy paper clip to you. Even worse, my Ph.D. may mean absolutely nothing to you. A lousy, no-good, spoiled, can't-give-it-away gefilte fish nothing to you. But again, you probably don't have a Ph.D. Do they call you doctor? All right, so maybe you do have a Ph.D. But mine is in psychology. That's all I'll say about that. I'm really not trying to show you up or appear self-important. It's just that I wrote this book. What I'm saying here is that I spent 12 years in college studying human behavior, social and behavior science, religious studies and philosophy.

The disciplines I studied taught me a lot about human behavior. Think about it, 12 years of studying human beings, what they are all about and why we do the things we do. Let me tell you now, there's an awful lot to know about why human beings do what they do, why they don't always get along with each other, and why some prefer plain brown M&Ms. I've got theories to explain these phenomena. I know what you're thinking. It took 12 years of college and thousands of dollars to learn why people prefer plain brown M&Ms. Listen, there's more to it. I've got some fancy theories to explain human behavior. Now, some people resist change because they like what's comfortable. Although there's nothing wrong with eating plain brown M&Ms for a lifetime, I'd ask why not consider a red M&M? If they ate the red M&M then they would have enriched their lives. In other words, they would have changed by being tolerant. I know, what enrichment is there to gain from eating a plain red M&M? Remember, it's just a metaphor and it's relevant to our discussion about enrichment. And don't say it didn't do anything. We'll talk later about how they were affected by this experience.

The other equally important thing I'd like you to understand is my credibility and legitimate authority on the subject of diversity. I'll tell you why later. All right, I'll explain why now. I think that this reading process will engage you in a meaningful way, and you'll trust that what I'm writing about has a great potential to raise your level of awareness about cultural diversity. You don't have to trust me about anything else. I will however, make a high-level self-disclosure here. I am a very trustworthy person, except of course when money is involved. All right, even when money is involved. So, what's the purpose of this book? If you meet me here with some degree of openness, despite all of the perceived effects of your cultural programming, we're going to achieve lots together. Your alter ego will also achieve lots. Now I'll discuss my credibility and legitimate authority on the subject of diversity. I just am, and you'll have to trust me. Period.

Learning to Think Critically

Listen, we're going to spend a few hours together, and you're going to learn a lot about cultural awareness and other things. You've probably realized by now that I'm not arrogant, pushy, irritating, emotionally constricted, or self-promoting. As a teacher, and I've been teaching about 15 years now, my goal is to get students to think critically about things. I want you to know that when I teach theories of personality development, I present all of the theories in an objective, balanced way, never trying to get students to conform to my way of thinking, even though my way of thinking is the right way. That's a joke. I don't indoctrinate. I just want you to make decisions that are well informed, where you make conclusions based on a careful weighing of the material presented to you. The reason you need to come to your own conclusions is because popular culture usually promotes distorted or inaccurate ideas about the truth. So, if you want to know the truth, learn to think critically. The alternative is shallow thinking.

For our purposes, I want you to learn more about why you think the way you do about other cultures. If you are biased about other cultures not living right, then let's examine how you developed your biases. The great psychologist William James put it pretty well when he said, "A great many people think they are thinking when they are merely rearranging their prejudices." You like that? My hope is you'll discover some interesting things about yourself during this challenging process. I guess you've learned by now that you, and only you can control your thinking. Your alter ego doesn't control your thinking. I don't control your thinking. I pretty much think that you control your thinking about things worth thinking about that could change your thinking about them.

My job here is to present this important material to you in a way that starts this process of thinking critically. It's like giving you the starter kit. You like that? One of the most important concepts we'll be studying is called cultural relativity, which is the understanding that we can't judge the behavior of other cultures, their cultural values, how they choose to live, and their rituals and customs, by comparing them to our culture.

Open-Mindedness

Listen, I'm not incredibly to the left or right when it comes to thinking about things. I have an open mind, very few problems and I've done well up until this time in my life in this society. I know my thinking can be constrained because of the many years of entrenchment in a cultural-bound value system that has served me well. I refer to my socialization process as cultural programming or cultural encapsulation.

Again, despite this confidence in my system, I'm coming to you with an open mind.

I suppose not being on the left or the right means I'm in the middle. But what does being in the middle really mean when it comes to taking a position on issues? Again, it depends on a lot of variables that could potentially influence how I think and feel about issues. The variables I'm talking about are gender, age, race, culture, and religious affiliation. See what I mean? One's culture, core values or their religious convictions can influence their attitude about issues. So, now what? I'm a level-headed thinker. I like to be level with people and always in a respectful way. I'm not going to define level headedness because the definition will be relative to my culture, ethnic group and my religious affiliation. This is what I mean when it comes to labeling people and trying to predict how they'll think about things. It just all depends on individual, personal factors.

Now, I'm not going to assign myself a label to identify my political affiliation, how I feel about certain social problems and issues, which thrift store I buy my clothes from or which topical ointment I use for my severe and persistent itch. You see, disclosing this information could bias how you feel about me. I will share this with you. I've always been much more interested in determining how the labels we assign each other limit or constrain our thinking about social problems and issues. So, let's not apply labels to each other and concentrate more on *who* we are rather than *what* we are. Focusing on who we are more accurately expresses our humanity, empathy, concern and generosity for others. Identifying what we are, like being a Republican, Democrat, Conservative or Liberal categorizes each of us into a box, assigning all sorts of behaviors that are consistent with that label. Well, that's all I'm going to say about that for now.

Look, I'm Jewish and you may be Christian, Hindu, Buddhist, or maybe an atheist. This situation shouldn't interfere with our capacity to live as friendly, accepting and caring neighbors. However, if we begin to argue about the truthfulness of Jesus being both G-d and man, as Christians believe and Jews reject, it will only divide us. If you're an atheist, I need to respect your view that there exists no such reality as G-d. It doesn't necessarily mean you can't have any of my gefilte fish. We can eat gefilte fish, herring and lox on a bagel together and have good breakfast conversation. And I won't serve you the four-day old bagels I can buy heavily discounted at the bagel place. I'll get us the fresh bagels and pay full price. So, instead of arguing about who G-d is and whose religion is true and right, I'd rather focus on how Judaism and Christianity functions in each of our lives to make us better human beings; how each faith obligates us to perform acts of kindness in the world.

The Author's Ph.D. in Psychology

Now, the last thing I need to mention is I have a Ph.D. in Psychology. I know I mentioned it earlier, but you might have forgotten it. So, here's an innocuous reminder to further substantiate my scholasticism, credibility and legitimate authority on the subject. You like that word scholasticism? A *scholasticist* is someone who practices scholarly things. It's what I do. I know, you've got the equivalent of a Ph.D. in social intelligence and it's served you incredibly well in life. I mean, isn't that the reaction people have when you tell them you've got a Ph.D.? Is it possible for me to have social intelligence and a Ph.D.? Let me remind you, I'm not one of those awkward and odd-looking academic types that hasn't spent time in your backyard. I've got lots of common sense and social intelligence. I've been to Home Depot, gone down the plumbing and electrical aisles a bunch of times now. I've looked at drill bits and replaced toilet seats in my house. I'd know what to do if I was the first guy to spot a fire in the theatre. I also know the interpretations of lots of proverbs. Listen, I've written proverbs and aphorisms for others to interpret. All right, I'll stop now. Sorry.

Looking for Enrichment

I hope you're open to looking at your long-held cultural assumptions, biases, and stereotypes in a realistic and honest way. If you are willing to challenge some of your conventional thoughts and perceptions about things, you'll get something out of this book. I know there are individuals who aren't interested in learning how to appreciate other cultures and how this experience can enrich their lives. You may not need any enriching experiences; you've had enough enrichment in your life. Can you tap out on enriching experiences in life? If life enrichment is like everything else, in that you can get too much, maybe you've had enough. I know, there are limits to things; it just depends what things. Things means you, of course. So, it depends on you.

I think you should seek out experiences that enrich your life. If you don't agree, then you're pretty much satisfied with the price you paid for your life, and the quality of life that came with it. I know, you got a great deal on it at an exclusive, incredibly high-end store that sells great lives; no upgrading with enrichment is necessary. Another way to look at enrichment is to see it as adding special accessories to your life. You like that? And like anything else, you've got to work and pay for the accessories. Remember, though, you'll look great with all the accessories. All right, you look awfully good without the accessories, too.

Enrichment can improve your life. So, why not go for the enrichment. Are you just too busy for enrichment? You prefer a simple, uncomplicated, functional, and predictable life. It's kind of like Herb who's been a security officer at the same big pickle plant for 46 years. No promotions or transfers in 46 years. Herb was probably really satisfied with his job and there's absolutely nothing wrong with him working at the big pickle plant for 46 years. It's just something to think more about. Herb clearly established job stability, security, and, well, that's about it. He also enjoyed some of the associated fringe benefits of the job, such as taking home lots of pickles and barrels.

Look, maybe I'm confusing you with your neighbor Hank whose life needs enriching. Maybe Hank is the enrichment deprived, real working fella I'm talking about. But I'm not talking about Hank. Why do you talk about Hank? I'm talking about you right now. Do me a favor, think about enrichment and whether you need more of it in your life, especially the higher level enrichment experiences. An enrichment experience won't pull you out of your life element. You won't end up becoming someone you don't want to be. Trust me. Enrichment will undoubtedly add another dimension to your life. You'll accessorize your life. You'll keep your current friends, job, and you won't turn into me. Your alter ego will also get enriched if you seek enrichment experiences. You can trust me here because money isn't involved.

Enrichment can also be seen as an experience human beings strive for in their quest to be all that they can possibly become in their lifetime. One of my favorite theorists is Abraham Maslow, a Humanistic Psychologist. Maslow theorized that human beings were born with an inherent capacity to be kind, generous and caring. His conception of human beings was positive and optimistic. According to Maslow:

> *Growth is, in itself, a rewarding and exciting process...the fulfilling of yearnings and ambitions...the acquisition of admired skills...the steady increase of understanding about people: the development of certain creativeness in whatever field, or most important, simply the ambition to be a good human being."*

Well, what do you think? Isn't that a nice way of looking at what enrichment or growth can do for you? As long as you're not afraid to challenge yourself to explore other cultures and lifeways, you'll profit from the experience. You really will. This learning opportunity could represent your ultimate enrichment experience, a fulfillment of your fullest inner potential to understand other cultures and people for the purpose of improving your cultural relations with other people. It's sort of like discovering more things about yourself. What you might learn about yourself by reading this book are your hidden prejudices and biases and how they distort your perceptions of other cultures.

Look, for $13.00 you have the potential to walk away from this book knowing yourself so much more; really understanding your motives, emotions and where you fall short on some things. Well, maybe falling short on just one thing. Sorry now, but everyone falls short on things. I'm pleased that you're courageous enough to explore why you fall short, where you fall short, how falling short influences your relationships with people, and why you're a short individual. Just kidding. I really don't know if you're short. Imagine freeing yourself up from the biases and prejudices you have about other cultures as a result of doing this work with me. I know you'd be awfully proud of yourself if you could achieve this noble, personal goal. I'd pretty much be real proud of you. Okay, not pretty much. I would be really proud of you.

Let's think about us. We're going to be together for a while now. Indulge me here and trust that I know what I'm talking about. And don't indulge me because you think I'm the poor, unassuming fella who needs to be right to feel better about himself. I don't need that kind of indulging or validation. I'm secure about my abilities and a bunch of other important things. Let me ask you something. What does enrichment mean to you and what kinds of things enrich your life? Let's start with a definition of enrichment. **Enrichment** means adding value, richness, or depth to something. For our purposes, we're talking about adding value or richness to your life. Now, you may not be interested in adding value to your life. I think that some people will ask themselves, "What does he mean by adding value to my life?" before they go for the enrichment. You might think that adding value to your life means you become more important. Well, you kind of do. You become more interesting because you add another dimension to your identity. It's like the more enriching experiences you have in life, the more opportunities you have to connect with other people who have had similar enrichment experiences. I'll make a sort of high-level self-disclosure to you now. In all the years I worked in inpatient psychiatric hospitals, I always took advantage of attending training opportunities to develop additional skills. Isn't that nice? These opportunities represented enrichment experiences that made me an important and sort of indispensable employee. Well, it did for a little while. I'm not sure I needed to make this high-level self-disclosure right now.

Don't you want to connect with other people? All right, maybe not all the time, but sometimes you do, and I know it depends on certain things, like who the people are. Would you want to connect with me? I'm really not strange. I've got two friends, I can hold a job and I have the social skills required to start, maintain and end a conversation. I won't look over your shoulder at other people when I'm talking to you. I'll buy you a birthday present that's not on sale, which means I'll pay full price. I'm really All right. I teach for a university. I'm told that I'm in very good standing in the neighborhood. People don't usually avoid me. If I call someone with caller ID, they usually pick up and talk to me. Is that enough for you to like me? I think your alter ego would like me and you wouldn't have to control your alter ego and insist that he or she like me. Being a psychologist has a lot to do with me being like-able. It's also enabled me to identify and utilize my fullest human potential in this world as compared to another world. You really shouldn't have any concerns about me. My past employers shouldn't have had any concerns about me.

Enrichment can allow you to grow. It might mean acquiring a new skill or something. It can also make you feel and look important. I don't need to work at feeling important because it comes to me quite naturally, and I already look important. At least that's what people I come into contact with tell me. Again, I'm not needing to feel self-important. It's just the feedback I get from others. You know, about looking important. And don't be asking yourself who these people are that say I look important.

Adding Value to Your Life

So what does adding value mean? Adding value to your life means enriching your life. Enrichment means you bring more depth and meaning to any relationship or situation. It's like you knowing more about certain things because of your increased fund of knowledge. People like impressing others with their fund of knowledge. In case you don't know, increased fund of knowledge is a euphemism for knowing a lot of things. I know some people who harbor an endless desire to impress others with their perceived fund of knowledge. Notice I said their "perceived" fund of knowledge. And no, I'm not one of those people. It's a perception people have about themselves, you know, that they have a great fund of knowledge.

Adding value also means opening yourself up to new experiences in life. It's adding richness and culture to your life. You might lead a basic, simple and functional life, which to others, may appear to be a non-enriched life. Yes, there's nothing wrong with that lifestyle. However, if you approach me and ask me how you can enrich your life, I might suggest that you try Sushi. Have you ever wanted to eat Sushi? Well, maybe not squid or octopus, but would you consider a California Roll because you can eat the avocado, cucumber and rice in it? See, you may have never considered going to a Sushi bar to eat a California Roll until I told you about it. There are probably at least three other people in California who aren't aware that they can order a California Roll at a Sushi bar. And who knows, there are probably other items on that Sushi bar menu you can eat instead of raw squid or octopus. There's eel, too.

This experience is an example of increasing your fund of knowledge. Is this enrichment? Is this adding value? Well, it is. You know why? Because you opened yourself up to a new experience. In addition, you've probably got a friend that's been trying to get you to eat at his or her favorite Sushi bar. I've got one of these friends. Everyone's got one of these kinds of friends. There's some plant in the City of Commerce that manufactures friends who like to get their friends to eat at Sushi bars. I wish they'd shut down this plant.

Anyway, the point I'm trying to make is that now you can go eat Sushi with your friend. This is what I mean by enrichment. You enriched your life by exposing yourself to Sushi. You also discovered another way to spend time with your friend. By the way, a real good friend of mine loves Sushi. About two years ago she took me to her favorite Sushi restaurant and introduced me to Sushi. I had some of the Sushi with the cooked shrimp and other cooked seafood and it was great. It was just expensive. Now, I get to spend more time with her when she's in town. I hope she doesn't read this, but I can only be with her for so long eating Sushi. I can only be with her for so long, period. I wanted to take her to some lousy buffet that serves Sushi. She declined and we ended up at her favorite, expensive Japanese restaurant.

Other Enrichment Opportunities

Let's see, what other kinds of things could represent enrichment experiences? How about joining a short story reading group. This activity will undoubtedly enrich your life. Reading great literature and analyzing the read for the deeper meaning will enable you to learn a little more about yourself, depending of course on what your take of the read is all about and the depth of your analysis. You see, there's a reason for you having the reaction you did to a short story. If you're able to analyze the story by understanding who the protagonist and antagonist are, and what external or internal conflicts the main character experiences, or how plots surface, then you'll sort of understand yourself better. It's like analyzing your reaction to the story. In general, reading classics is not only an enriching experience, but is a mind-opening adventure, which in a larger way will help you begin to understand your life and place in the world. There's not much else beyond your life and place in the world. That pretty much takes care of me. I don't know about you, but once I know why I'm here, like this certain place, and why I'm doing what it is I'm doing, I feel more secure and needed in the world. I'm also sure my alter ego will feel more secure in the world. Anyway, that's how I see it. And no, I'm not trying to get you to see it like me. You probably don't want to ever think like me. By the way, sharing things about myself with you is considered a self-disclosure. I don't like to make too many high-level self-disclosures to people I don't know really well.

Have you ever considered taking a class on hot-air ballooning and what it's all about? Or a class on how to go ghost hunting? How about more conventional, personal enrichment classes, such as stained glass painting, beginning photography, or learning about outdoor adventures. How about stargazing? I'm talking about gazing at stars in the sky and not in Hollywood. All of these classes will generate some self-discovery and personal growth. If you take these self-growth experiences seriously, you'll experience a renewed, enlarged and creative sense of self. So, why aren't you driving the hot rod or working as an auctioneer at a cattle auction? Just think of all the possible places you could have ended up at, and try to figure out why you're right here at this time in your great life. Did some mysterious social force lead you to this place or are you a self-directed person that decides where you go?

2

Hey Pal, We Don't Do That Around Here. Where Are you From?

o o o o o o o o o o o o o o o o o o o o o o o o o o o o o

"The true civilization is where every man gives to every other every right that he claims for himself."

—Robert Green Ingersoll

"If men would consider not so much wherein they differ, as wherein they agree, there would be far less uncharitableness and angry feeling in the world"

—Joseph Addison

"Life is the art of drawing sufficient conclusions from insufficient premises"

—Samuel Butler

Understanding cultural diversity will take work if you decide to do something about it. It's like taking a leap of action. Ever take a leap of action? I know people talk about taking a leap of faith. I've taken many leaps of faith and well, we can talk later about premature and unsuccessful leaps of faith. A leap of action means pushing the launch button and launching. You can't stay on the launch pad for 32 years. The fuel goes bad and sometimes you forget where the launch button is. Even if you find the launch button, you may forget where you're supposed to go, you know, your launch destination. Do you still want to go to the same place after 32 years?

To work means you will make a serious commitment to think in a deep way that generates awareness. Let me tell you something. Acquiring awareness, especially the new creative, breakthrough kind I'm talking about, is worth the $13.00 you spent on this book because it will add greater meaning, depth and value to your life. Isn't that nice now? Imagine adding **depth** to your life. It's about other people experiencing you as substantive, thoughtful and insightful. **Substantive** means having real substance to your thinking and being. You know, deeper than the first pancake on the stack. You have to admit acquiring awareness means knowing more about what motivates your behavior and understanding your emotions. And there's no denying that knowledge is valuable information for your dash. One person's life on earth is just a dash compared to the life of the earth. A 50-yard dash. Remember running 50-yard dashes in your junior high physical education classes? I don't want to brag or anything, but I had one of the fastest times in my school.

Look, I know it's a lousy deal, but why agonize about the dash? I think the more knowledge you possess, the more enriched your dash will be. Thinking about our dash means reflecting on the time span of our dash in relation to how long earth has been around. How's it feel now? A lousy 50-yard dash is about all we're going to run in this lifetime. I know, I shouldn't be so presumptuous thinking this is the only dash we'll ever experience. How about our alter egos, are they in the same dash as us? Since we're discussing our time-limited existence on earth, compared to anywhere else, I thought you'd like to know what Albert Einstein had to say about our dash:

> *Strange is our situation here on earth. Each of us comes for a short visit, not knowing why, yet seeming to divine a purpose. From the standpoint of daily life, however, there is one thing we do know: that people are here for the sake of other people, for the countless souls with whose*

*fate we are connected by a bond of sympathy. Many times a day I real-
ize how my own outer and inner life is built upon the labors of others,
both living and dead, and how earnestly I must exert myself in order to
give in return, as much as I have received, and am still receiving."*

All right, you're pretty much committed to this read now. The
$5.00 read. Oh, I'm sorry, you paid $13.00 for my book. The other
nice people got it for $5.00. Are you regretting the purchase? If you
ever took an Introduction to Marketing class, you'd have learned that a
phenomenon called "Post Purchase Cognitive Dissonance" occurs
when you buy something you shouldn't have bought. Do you have
"Post Purchase Cognitive Dissonance?" Listen, it's okay to admit that
you have this problem. I'm sorry you're feeling this way though. I
mean, "Post Purchase Cognitive Dissonance" is just a fancy way of saying you shouldn't have spent the $13.00 on my book. If it's really
bothering you to the extent you're starting to miss work, experience a
diminished ability to think, have recurrent thoughts of death, a diminished interest or pleasure in most or all activities of your life, or are suf-
fering from insomnia and weight loss, then let me know so we can talk
about how to get you feeling better about your purchase of my book.
I'd be open to talking to you about this problem. But remember, all
sales are final. Sorry. Listen, there's lots of other things you've purchased in your life that created "Post Purchase Cognitive Dissonance"
and you probably paid a whole lot more than the lousy $13.00 you
spent on my book. Would you have "Post Purchase Cognitive Dissonance" if you paid $5.00 for the book?

Challenging Your Cultural Assumptions

Exploring diversity means challenging yourself to examine your
strongly held cultural assumptions about people from different cultures. Do you like challenging yourself? Seriously asking yourself why
you think or feel a certain way about people? You see, your cultural
assumptions about other people comes from what you read, hear in the

media and what others say about people. You may have never had any meaningful opportunities to interact with people from other cultures. Thus, you're at a loss if you've never had any encounters with other cultures, and are left with second-hand accounts or impressions of others. I bet the impressions formed were probably quick and oversimplified perceptions. Ask yourself: Do I have any oversimplified assumptions of people from other cultures? I wonder what oversimplified assumptions you have about me? I'll make a high-level self-disclosure now, there's pretty much nothing oversimplified about me. I'm not saying I'm complicated to figure out, just that there's lots of depth and substance to me.

Imagine if your assumptions about any culture were misperceptions, and you weren't aware they were inaccurate perceptions. If no one brought this to your attention, your inaccurate perceptions would influence your interactions with individuals from this culture. The potential problem here is that your misperception is probably an unfavorable one, and it would bias your thoughts and feelings in a negative way. So, when it's time to interact with this culture, your biased perceptions will influence your interactions. In other words, your interactions with individuals in this culture will be colored by the negative stereotypes you had about their life ways.

Do you want to engage in this confusing and potentially aggravating exercise at this time in your life? You know, checking out your cultural assumptions? Why not? You already spent the money on this book, which you'll have for a whole lifetime now. You could loan it to somebody, but that's a missed sale for me. Don't loan the book to anybody. Just tell them to call the "Thinking on Things Institute" to purchase their own copy. Thanks now.

Have you ever checked your biased perceptions of a culture which you acquired from some other source, against an actual experience you've had with a member of that same culture? Well, what happened? Your perceptions were either accurate or inaccurate. I'm hoping your biased perceptions, when compared to your actual experience, were inaccurate. If so, then applaud yourself for modifying your cultural perceptions of the culture. I mean, are you going to modify them or will you wait a little bit? Why don't you do both? Either modify or don't modify your perceptions and keep interacting with people in that culture to see what unfolds. Listen, this process of modifying perceptions and holding them for a while as we continue to interact with others is incredibly valuable. Remember now, if you don't check your assumptions against reality, they become biases, which can result in stereotypical behavior and prejudice.

Let's summarize this stuff. The human mind likes to process information efficiently by categorizing it and making generalizations and conclusions based on limited evidence or experience. The limited information and evidence refers to the lack of many firsthand experiences we have when we think and act on cultural assumptions about others. We discussed how human beings prefer what looks familiar to what looks unfamiliar.

Pursuing the Ultimate Enrichment Experience

Now, if you're truly interested in gaining firsthand experiences of other cultures, you'll probably feel apprehensive and anxious spending time in the culture. It's because differences between cultures are sometimes seen as threatening. What you'll first discover is that you focus on the differences rather than the similarities between the two cultures. It's just a human tendency. A sort of unconscious, automatic reaction. We tend to see problems in others before we see them in ourselves. This explains why you're thinking that I have lots of problems right now. If you are aware of your behavior, you'll monitor your degree of apprehension and notice how solid your cultural identity is during this process of experiencing another culture firsthand. Look, there's no escaping the ever-present vulnerability we all experience in life. I think whenever we're in situations that require us to seriously look at other ways of life, we automatically feel apprehensive. It's a sort of instinctual response to observing otherness. What do you think?

Are you ready for an enrichment experience? I'm talking about a very high-level enrichment experience. If you're in the mood to be introduced to new angles on life, other cultures and their culture bound values, and to be challenged, then now is the time to push the launch button and launch. A week or month from now won't work. Sixteen years from now certainly wouldn't be a good time. Apathy could paralyze you. You could develop an anxiety disorder. Worse, you could be diagnosed with "Button Resistant Disorder," an anxiety problem preventing you from pushing the launch button. So, let's do it now and not argue about it. You may never be in this mood again. Capitalize on this moment. Think about all the moods available to you. There are so many other moods, like the mood to fill your car with gas, swim a mile, or go outdoor bass fishing. Ever wonder why they call it outdoor bass fishing? Can you go indoor bass fishing? Just something to think more about later. These are serious temptations; they are competing moods that have the potential to derail you. Know what I mean? You can swim tomorrow. You like that word *derail?* I think it's the appropriate word to describe what could happen if you allow some mysterious social force to alter your mood and interfere with your pursuit of the ultimate enrichment experience.

Think about the wonderful benefits of enlarging and appreciating your view of things. Who knows what you might discover about yourself and the world. This process could generate some insight that you otherwise would never enjoy. Trust me, insight is a good thing. It's better than sleeping in until 4:00 p.m. on a Monday when you're off work, waking up in time to watch Monday Night Football and being served five pounds of Cajun marinated jumbo shrimp in a basket. It's because insight lasts a whole lifetime, unless you lose it, of course. Can you lose insight?

So, What is Insight?

Insight is incredibly valuable. Insight into oneself means understanding your emotions and motives. Now, you know that some individuals don't understand what motivates their behavior or why they feel a certain way about things. In other words, these individuals haven't spent enough time getting to know themselves well enough to predict how they might behave in certain situations. If they were insightful, they could anticipate how they would behave in social or interpersonal situations.

Insight could create a life-transforming experience that leads you to achieve your fullest human enrichment potential. Get a load of that now. Wouldn't that be worth the lousy money you paid for this book? You could experience something like an epiphany and have a breakthrough enrichment experience filled with enduring meaning and value for you. How do you like that? Yes, enduring, instructive, lifelong value. It's just a fancy way of saying this enrichment experience will stay with you for the entire dash. It's sort of like your social security number providing you with lifelong identification. I didn't say your social security number would provide you with enduring, lifelong meaning and value. Marriage and good topical ointments give your life meaning and purpose.

Listen, sorry if I'm aggravating you. Remember this important thing. Things could be a whole lot worse. I mean it now. Imagine being tested on Sartre's "Being and Nothingness." It's 768 pages of the most dreadful, painstaking and complex analysis of human consciousness. Just when you thought consciousness simply meant you knew you existed, and were aware that you could breathe, think, feel and fill your car up with gas. Well, you're right. It's just that it takes some people longer to explain how they know they're alive. Here's a worse situation. How about being married to me? What do you think? If you were married to me, I wouldn't always be reminding you that your existence has no meaning, that there's no good reason for why you and I exist and I wouldn't be asking you to prove that you're alive. We'd talk about other things like Neil Young, my Vanagon, Schizophrenia, the beat poets Kerouac and his buddies Ernest Hemingway, Franz Kafka and Albert Camus. Kafka and Camus are my favorite existential writers.

Diversity and the Pull for Sameness

Now we can discuss diversity and the other incredibly important stuff you need to know. I know, there are people who have no desire to open themselves up to diversity. Sure am glad you're open. So, what happened to openness? These individuals probably aren't aware that they may be stuck in rigid, relatively undesirable, habitual patterns of thinking and perceiving. I mean, they just don't have the desire or awareness you and I have concerning the value of thinking about things differently. So, they end up ignoring and not appreciating cultural differences in their world. At least you have the desire to learn about different cultures and how their culture-bound values lead to different life ways.

Look, it's easy to be oblivious to the blatant differences in others. If someone looks different, talks a strange language, doesn't eat at Hometown Buffet and their behavior doesn't affect you, we tend to let it go. It's sort of like their behavior is innocuous. After you notice these differences, it's easy to not do anything about it, like think about why it's different. We don't usually think much about this person's culture and his/her value system. We're not thinking about how their different life orientation to the world affects how they interact with you. So, in the end, you're left thinking about whether that individual is eventually going to change and be like you. I think we'd like them to change and be like us. You might disagree with me here, but I think we have a tendency to want everything to look the same, including people. What do you think?

Acculturation

There is actually a fancy word to describe what we're discussing here. It's called **acculturation**. Individuals from different cultures living in the United States, which I'll refer to as the dominant society, have to think about their social identities. I mean, no one should expect individuals from different cultures to abandon their ethnic identity and heritage in their new country. People from different cultures need to retain close identification with their religious and ethnic groups and, depending on their needs, they can simultaneously identify with and integrate themselves into the new, dominant culture. Integrating into the new, dominant culture means adopting the values, language and customs of the new culture. It may also include interacting with the dominant culture's public and private institutions.

Now, like everything else in the world, there are differing levels of acculturation. There are individuals who comfortably alternate between their heritage and the dominant culture. Individuals in this category don't necessarily assert a preference for one culture over the other. And, of course, there are people who have problems balancing their value systems against the dominant culture's value system, making it difficult for them to interact comfortably in their new environment.

People find comfort in having things look and stay the same, meaning people pretty much look alike and behave similarly in these familiar surroundings. It confirms that you're doing the right things and that you are in the right place. It gives you comfort to know you're not too different from your friends. I suppose the logical conclusion you'd make is that everybody must be doing the right things because we can't all be wrong in thinking and behaving in similar ways. Can we? Have you ever thought about the possibility that all of you are doing the wrong thing? Probably not. So, deviating from the habitual ways of thinking and behaving is taking a risk at appearing different and having people talk about you. And no, people don't talk about me because I'm different. If they talk about me it's because of other things. I'm going to stop now. It's still sort of early to be making more high-level self-disclosures.

I'll tell you something now, instead of later. It's comforting and reassuring to look around and see things that look familiar to you; people who dress like you, worship like you and talk like you. Think about it. If you're the only one wearing an expensive looking cowboy hat, alligator-skin cowboy boots, Wrangler jeans with a western shirt, and you're in a psychiatrist's waiting room in Beverly Hills, people will be looking at you. I mean, they'll look at you. They will certainly be looking you up, down and all around. Imagine if you were a Chinese male in that cowboy attire in the psychiatrist's waiting room. Lots of people would be talking about you now. I'd even be talking about you. All right, so I won't talk about you.

I'll end this subject with a discovery I made years ago. I entered an elementary school classroom and saw a poster on the wall that nicely explained what I'm discussing with you here. The poster read something like "Be at the right place, the right time, doing the right thing, with the right people." That's it. Now you know what I mean. I know, there's nothing wrong with teachers expecting obedient and respectful behavior from their students. It's just an example of how our culture sometimes demands consistency and conformity of behavior in certain situations.

Culture

What about the term culture? **Culture** is what members of a certain society share, things like beliefs, values, norms, language, art, music, and even material objects the culture produces. Things like Pepto Bismol, condensers, U-Joints, and antibacterial soap are examples of material objects. Other objects include forklifts, a drill press, anvil, and brussel sprouts. These are things needed by people to sustain their cultures. There are also occupations like a vector inspector, plumber or lawyer. Admit it now. You thought I was going to say something disparaging about lawyers. Why would I do that? I've got one very good friend who is a lawyer. I also have other good friends who aren't lawyers. My lawyer friend is genuinely nice, and he's just a naturally caring, funny, very intelligent, unassuming, very likeable and respectful individual. It's not like you'd have to work hard to like him. You'd like him right away if you met him. You know, there's lots more I could write about him, but I forgot his name now. I'm not going to say any more about him except that he embodies what a good human being is all about. In other words, there's nothing wrong with him and he's a lawyer. Can you imagine that?

Now, ***cultural objects*** and ***artifacts*** developed as a result of a culture using technology. These items fulfill a human purpose. Think about it. Could you and I live without Motrin, pacemakers, or U-Joints? Thinking about it doesn't necessarily mean I'm going to think about it for you and give you my thoughts. Culture is everything that human beings create together, including their society and the institutions to create social order. How do you like that? Without social order little would be possible. Imagine living in a society with no social order. You could walk into your favorite thrift shop and pick out all the clothes and other hot items you desperately need and not pay for them. Without social order lots would be possible because the norms guiding our behavior are absent. Sociologists call this kind of social condition *anomie*. Just something for you to look up later. I think its *anomie*.

How about the shared belief that individuals who jeopardize our safety should be separated from the general population by being incarcerated? Or, that to continue paying rent or mortgage you need to hold a job? Keeping a job is called job stability. The people I live with are always reminding me to maintain job stability. For some ridiculous reason, they think I've jeopardized my job stability several times. Can you imagine that? I don't want to say much more about it right now. It would just aggravate me when I'm feeling reasonably well. The medicine I'm taking is working well these days. By the way, I just made another high-level self-disclosure.

Language

A healthy, functioning society emerges when all of its members act on the elements of shared understanding to get on with the day-to-day living. As a result, acceptable patterns of behavior are established. Think of culture as a group of people living in a natural setting, communicating with each other in comprehensible ways. Through **_language_** we create shared symbols, knowledge, and the foundations of a society. Without language none of this would be possible. Animals communicate by certain sounds and gestures, and you and I communicate using symbolic language. The only reason we can communicate with each other is because we speak the same language. We have a shared understanding of our language that enables us to effectively communicate most of the time. Aren't you glad I have a written method allowing me to communicate with you right now?

Language enables us to communicate our thoughts and feelings, pity the poor M&Ms that actually can't communicate their thoughts and feelings. As much as I'd like them to, so I can further illustrate concepts with them, they can't talk (except on television). So, language, when expressed intelligibly, allows us to communicate with one another. You wouldn't be able to order caviar and onion rings from Big Lou's Volcano Burgers without language. As you can see, your life would be miserable if you couldn't effectively express your needs.

Types of Subcultures

A subculture can arise in a dominant society or culture. A subculture emerges when a group of people agrees to their own set of norms, values and beliefs, which are different from the dominant culture. You see, the subculture still shares certain elements of the dominant culture, but it has its own identity and little community. Religious groups like the Amish can be considered a subculture. The Hare Krishna is another religious subculture quite distinct in the way they dress; wearing robes, beads and shaving their heads. They also don't eat meat, which isn't so bad. Adolescents are a subculture because of the unique way they dress, talk, and behave. There are ***deviant subcultures*** such as terrorist groups, criminals and gangs. Obviously these groups' norms and values are unacceptable to the dominant culture. For starters, these deviant cultures don't treat all life as sacred. So, they wouldn't miss me if they did something to me and I stayed 46 forever. Staying 46 forever is just another way of saying I'd be dead. I wouldn't be around for the dash. My alter ego wouldn't be around either. I'd miss my alter ego. My alter ego would miss me. You'd miss me. Right? I mean, admit it now. Wouldn't you miss me a little bit? I'd miss you.

All right, don't tell me you didn't catch the "Yes Captain, I'm Awake" check three paragraphs ago. Have you ever ordered caviar from a fast food hamburger establishment? I'll tell you something now, Big Lou makes the ultimate charbroiled cheeseburger. Eating one of these cheeseburgers is an enrichment experience. By the way, I eat one cheeseburger a month and I don't ever supersize anything. Imagine being addicted to supersizing, that would be a major problem.

Knowledge, Beliefs and Values

The other elements of a culture are knowledge, beliefs and values. ***Knowledge*** refers to statements or theories that come from empirical evidence. Examples of widely established and commonly accepted statements that represent knowledge would be that there's gravity on earth or that human beings are mortal. How about that Einstein was a genius? So, cultural knowledge refers to those statements that are well known and shared by most everyone in the culture.

Beliefs are statements that aren't necessarily verifiable and cannot be proven to be true because they are commonly referred to as conventional wisdom. ***Conventional wisdom*** means that we accept the statement without questioning its truthfulness. It's like me claiming that Francine's Smorgasbord is better than Harry's Buffet. There's many of other examples of conventional wisdom.

How about the belief that there is an all-loving, merciful, and forgiving G-d that created human beings? Now, I know this is controversial, but I'm only using it as an example of a belief some people espouse. Let's add that the institution of religion is a belief. So, you should pretty much know by now that beliefs are ideas that are subjective and unverifiable. You like that word unverifiable? It means the belief's truthfulness can't be scientifically tested because there hasn't been a credible sighting of G-d lately. But then again, there are lots of people claiming to have seen and talked to G-d.

Values are very strongly held beliefs that typically originate from morality. Examples of values are justice, fairness, compassion, equality, openness, sharing, cooperation, and respect. The problem with values is that not everyone in a culture agrees on what is and isn't a value. For example, I know that for some people in our culture, getting ahead is valued. There is nothing wrong with that value. I refer to this value as part of the American dream that promotes and rewards achievement orientation. Interestingly, there are other cultures where competition and achievement orientation is discouraged and not valued. In other cultures, pursuing spiritual enlightenment is valued. Some cultures pursue harmony and balance in nature. I think you'll agree with me that ending someone's life against his or her will is immoral because all of us value life. In our mainstream, American culture, life is treated as sacred. However, sadly enough, there's always a potential for people in the same culture to not honor this value.

In our culture, values are sometimes expressed through proverbs. Here are a few examples of proverbs and the values they're supposed to reflect: Cleanliness is next to G-dliness (Cleanliness); You've made your bed, now lie in it (Responsibility, Personal Choices); Early to bed, early to rise (Diligence, Persistence); It's not whether you win or lose, but how you play the game (Good sportsmanship).

Now let's now discuss specific cultural values for the Hispanic, Asian and mainstream Caucasian, American culture. I'll list the value and how it is treated in each of the cultures.

Individual versus Family: In the Asian and Hispanic cultures, the family is emphasized more than the individual. In modern American culture, the individual is often emphasized more than the family. Individualism honors the uniqueness of each individual in his/her search for meaning in life. In contemporary mainstream Caucasian culture, individualism is usually expressed as achievement orientation motivated by self-interest, rather than a desire for collective involvement. Collective involvement is just a fancy way of saying the emphasis is on family and community instead of on the individual.

Time: For Asians, time is usually not specific and tends to flow like a stream. In the Hispanic culture time is vague and relative. In contemporary mainstream Caucasian culture time, is usually treated as precise and is divided into chunks, like hour by hour, which represents opportunities to produce something or to earn money. As you know, we thrive on using time efficiently to complete tasks.

Individualism and Expressive Individualism

I want to discuss *individualism* (here rather than somewhere else). Individualism originated in Western civilization in the 15th century. Individualism holds that life is sacred, and that human beings should be treated with dignity. Individualism also considers human beings as more important than society. Now, expressive individualism refers to the unique expression of an individual's feelings and thoughts. Expressive individualism most likely had its origins in the Romantic movement of the late eighteenth and early nineteenth centuries. *Romanticism* was a movement that rejected the scientific approach with its focus on reason and scientific inquiry to improve the human condition. The scientific approach generated a body of knowledge, which was used to understand the workings of our world. In other words, science was the primary method for human beings to control their destiny. However, science relied heavily on the use of our intellect and reason to dominate nature, making us overly confident that science was the only acceptable kind of knowledge.

Expressive individualism is about the basic goodness of human beings, and it stresses and emphasizes our emotional life, creativity, and imagination. It's about trusting your intuition on things in the world. In comparison to science, expressive individualism could lead to intuitive knowledge by de-emphasizing the importance of using our intellect and reason to understand our world. It focuses on how self-reflection can generate self-discovery. Self-reflection just means sitting and thinking about things. Expressive individualism nurtures self-realization, self-growth, and self-actualization. I wonder if these three concepts mean the same thing? What do you think?

One can argue that our culture focuses too much on how we feel and on nourishing the growth of our true self. I'm not sure about this. I've got to think more about it, and I'll get back to you later. All right, I'll think and discuss it with you now. Expressive individualism may deceptively encourage human beings to become too self-sufficient and self-reliant. It may encourage a pursuit of too much individual fulfillment and discourage individuals from making more serious connections to others, to society and to social institutions. One final thought for you to ponder. Is it possible for human beings to develop their genuine selves as they distance themselves from their cultural and social connections? By cultural and social connections I mean attachments to cultural and institutional anchors such as churches, synagogues, schools and colleges, museums, and cultural arts centers.

Harmonizing Religion and Science

At this point, I want to illustrate how the human tendency to polarize things can be problematic by juxtaposing religion and science. Let's start by defining religion as an institution with sociological functions. In sociological terms, religion is an institution that gives meaning to our lives through adherence to beliefs, morals, rituals, and other spiritual practices. These beliefs and practices were created by human beings in response to social forces they could not comprehend. It was primarily about believing in a reality way beyond the perceptible facts in our ordinary human experience, a sort of intuitive knowledge or faith. Emile Durkheim, one of the founders of sociology defined religion as:

> *"A unified system of beliefs and practices relative to sacred things,…which unite into one single moral community called a Church, all those that adhere to them."*

I think humans created religion, much like the institution of family, out of a need to impose meaning in their lives. If enough mysteries exist in our lives, we need to respond to this unknowable reality. So, religion provides us with ways of dealing with the unknown, invisible reality. Religion can create a sense of certainty in an otherwise very uncertain reality. That uncertain reality are experiences we cannot explain, such as untimely losses and the certainty of death. Religion lets us surrender our despair, fear, and anxiety to a sacred, transcendent, supernatural deity. It's what we all refer to as faith, which is usually part of our life orientation, a belief consisting of a world beyond what we can see. It's called the *ineffable*. It's just another fancy word. You can call it the stuff you don't quite get right now or maybe even later. Look, I'm still not getting it. But I know I've got more time left to understand what it is I'm supposed to get. Know what I mean?

Let's now discuss what science does for us. It does a lot. The realistic, objective assessment of our reality is what science gives humanity so nicely. Science enables us to obtain an understanding of the physical world; the world we can all see, touch, smell, taste, and hear. Science is the practice of gathering objective data, facts, and theories to help us control and predict the outcome of our lives and the occurrence of social events in the world. As a model for creating predictability in our lives, science is wonderful. It is an experimental process, a rational, methodical practice for understanding the mysteries of the world. I guess what we don't understand suggests there are limits to science or limits to man's intelligence. It's that ineffable thing again.

With regard to science and religion, the desired perspective is one that harmonizes both disciplines. In other words, the challenge is to assume an attitude that accommodates revelation and science. Now wouldn't that be really nice? Some people resist integrating them because we have a need to polarize things in the world; meaning you need an allegiance to one or the other. And some people rely less on religion for meaning in life and more on science and its great discoveries to increase their quality of life. How does this sound to you: Science teaches and explains how the world works and religion teaches us how to act, how to be moral, kind and loving human beings, how to determine what is and isn't important and what to pray for in the world. You can start by praying for good things in my life. I mean, I'd pray for good things in your life.

I suspect most religions represent humanity's search for meaning in life. Many of the world's faiths attempt to understand their spiritual reality named G-d. I think the creation of religion is a universal phenomenon. About 80 years ago, an anthropologist named Bronislaw Malinowski studied the tribal customs of the Trobriand Islanders, in addition to other tribes on a South Pacific Island. He noticed that the tribes performed different religious activities. For example, one tribe practiced a lot of magical rituals, while others performed little magic. Malinowski realized that one of the tribes lived near a calm lagoon where lots of fish were caught. So, his explanation for why this tribe performed fewer magical rituals was because they had lots of fish and there was no need for rituals to protect the fishermen when they went to fish at sea. The other tribe, sadly enough, often sent out their fishermen only to return with no fish. Malinowski concluded that the tribe that couldn't catch fish performed magical rituals to gain some control over uncertain social forces.

What's all of this interesting stuff supposed to mean for us? It means that when life is good and predictable, we are less anxious and fearful with less of a need for rituals. You probably knew that, didn't you? As humans accumulate knowledge and improve their ability to predict the outcome of their lives, there is less reliance on magic. What do you think? Another way of saying it is that when times are really good, some of us aren't praying and thanking G-d enough for the prosperity. Not that all of us need to thank G-d for our prosperity. We sort of forget about G-d then revive G-d when times aren't so prosperous. Know what I mean?

So, it looks like religion or faith provides us with ways of dealing with the unknown. Do you think religion is essential for human survival? Think about it now. You don't have to agree with me, of course. Well, you really can't agree with me because you don't know if I think religion is essential for human survival. I mean, I haven't told you my position on it yet. Think about the functions of religion again. The most important ones are how religion compels us to conform to the norms, values and morals of society. You know, the virtuous behaviors such as not lying, stealing or harming others. Research demonstrates that individuals who are religious are less likely to violate laws. In other words, they are not as likely to commit crimes and get into trouble with the law because most religions encourage their followers to be friendly, generous, moral and to obey the Golden Rule. Religion keeps us connected to a faith that defines who we are as people united by common, shared beliefs and values. It's a real important one because in modern society you can easily be identity-less. Is there such a word? Everyone needs an identity that they can strongly connect with and to be proud of, an identity to add meaning and purpose in life.

I hope this helped you understand how religion and science can be harmonized rather than polarized. We profit from discoveries made in medicine, biology, and from technological developments that ultimately improve the quality of our lives. But we need more than science to nourish our spiritual side. Religion is just as essential as science for human survival, giving us purpose and meaning in life, in addition to the moral codes to create a more peaceful and loving world. So, I guess now you know how I feel about whether we need religion for human survival. I think we pretty much do. Religion and science are not mutually exclusive. You can believe in both religion and science existing harmoniously and adding to our understanding of humanity. One is not better or more credible than the other.

Religious Tolerance

Since we're discussing religion and how it's related to intercultural awareness and tolerance, I think we should devote some time to discussing the functions of the different religions of the world. As you know by now, we must be tolerant of other faiths and religions of the world. Wars and major disputes can be attributed to the intolerance of competing faiths between neighboring countries. Historically, disputes between religions arose because people prayed to the wrong G-d. Do you know who the right G-d is? How do you know for sure? Why does there have to be one right G-d for everybody to pray to? And why do you insist that I pray to your G-d? Why won't you let me pray to my G-d, even when I don't profess my G-d is the right G-d? I'm not arguing with you about who the right G-d is.

If we can accept everyone's desire to worship their own G-d, and trust that their religion obligates them to be decent, kind and moral individuals, then why worry about how they'll treat you? Instead of worrying about who the one, right G-d is, let's celebrate everyone's religion and understand how their faith functions in their life to make them decent, loving, ethical and moral human beings. How do you feel about that line of thinking? We discussed earlier the need to focus on how religion functions in people's lives. Christianity, Judaism, Islam, and Hinduism are loving faiths encouraging its followers to honor the Golden Rule. You know, most of the world's faiths have some form of the Golden Rule. Does that make you feel better about humanity now? I think we should understand how religion functions in people's lives rather than which people are praying to the one, righteous and right G-d.

Inclusion, Cultural Universals, Cultural Diversity and Cultural Relativity

Now, what about *diversity*? For starters, we can illustrate diversity with our example of the one green M&M, one blue M&M, and one orange M&M living with a bunch of plain brown M&Ms in their community. This situation represents diversity. Beyond this definition, diversity means providing recognition and, well, here's that fancy word, inclusion of the thoughts and feelings of all members of a society. *Inclusion* means that people from all backgrounds, including racial, ethnic, and cultural backgrounds, have an equal opportunity to share their thoughts with the larger culture, and that they can belong, achieve, and contribute to the larger society without being discriminated against. Can you imagine living in such an ideal society?

I think people who ignore how diversity can enrich their life are fearful of stepping out of their circle. The circle represents their comfort zones. These people take comfort being around others who look, think, and talk similarly. I don't know about you, but I welcome diversity. Why do some people get anxious working alongside individuals who look different and have their own beliefs, values and spiritual longings? I'll tell you now, and with absolute certainty, that you cannot catch their cultural virus. I know I'm right here. As long as you are secure in your cultural and ethnic identity, then you shouldn't feel threatened by the otherness you observe in that person working next to you. Think about it now.

I think all of us agree that some *cultural universals* exist in the world. And no, seeing a McDonalds in Salzburg is not considered a cultural universal. All sorts of human beings occupy this planet and they sustain their civilization and culture. We're all biological organisms with general needs that must be met in order for us to survive. These basic needs are pretty much biological ones such as food, safety and shelter. The cultural universals I'm describing are the human need for communication, love, acceptance, health, sex, belongingness, religion, and art. These elements are actually the things that constitute a culture; the necessities of human social life. I think we can all agree that these cultural universals are found in any group referring to itself as a culture.

Not everyone shares the same thoughts about the important values, morals and beliefs of your culture. Your values are specific to you and your culture. So, *cultural diversity* also refers to that variety of ethnic, racial, religious, and individual characteristics of people in a particular society. Let me share something with you that will demonstrate how diverse our world is. Anthropologists report that the diversity of human cultures is so incredibly large that there are about 2,800 distinct languages in the world, and most of them have no words in common with the other languages.

After you realize that your culture is not culturally superior to any other culture, you'll understand *cultural relativity*. You see, all of those social scientists and anthropologists studying various cultures of the world discovered cultural relativity while evaluating the practices of the cultures they were observing. So, cultural relativity is the understanding that the behavior of a certain culture should not be evaluated based on another culture's standards. Most of the time, the behaviors of a culture that seem quite alien to us are consistent or in harmony with the rest of that culture. As you can see, culture must be understood on its own terms.

For me, *cultural relativism* means I'm willing to look, with an open mind, at other cultures and how their people live. Remember, try to approach situations with a degree of openness. What I want you to understand is that our socialization process constrains our thoughts; robbing us of our ability to understand and appreciate the diverse behaviors of other cultures. In the end, we become totally entrenched in our own behavior patterns and tend to automatically make negative evaluations of how other members of a culture behave.

3

"Hey, I Like the Plain Red M&Ms and Not the Yellow Ones"

o o o o o o o o o o o o o o o o o o o o o o o o o o o o o o o o o o

"In the real world, one is under the strongest compulsion to construe things one way or another"

—*Walker Percy*

"Few people can be happy unless they hate some other person, nation, or creed"

—*Bertrand Russell*

"If you hate a person, you hate something in him that is part of yourself. What isn't part of ourselves doesn't disturb us"

—*Hermann Hesse*

So you're not interested in trying the plain yellow M&M. You've probably got good reasons for refusing the yellow M&M. You've been eating the red ones a good long time now. Maybe you had a lousy experience eating a yellow M&M. Or someone told you that those plain yellow M&Ms didn't taste good and you've never challenged yourself to actually check it out. How do you like that? You lacked the courage to test your assumption that the poor plain yellow M&M didn't taste as good as the more desired plain red M&M.

Just remember, you've got to decide what you'll accept as truth or assumption, and since you're a mature and flexible-minded individual, I trust you'll make good decisions. Am I making an assumption that you're a mature, capable and flexible minded individual? Look, I know you are, because you are reading this book. You've just got to keep being tolerant about things; to have the courage to perceive things differently. If you modify your perceptions of the plain yellow M&M, you'd be willing to taste it and decide if it tastes differently than the plain red M&M. Maybe you're just reacting to the color yellow. Altering your perception will raise some anxiety in you, because you'd have to move out of your **comfort zone.** Your comfort zone only has plain red M&Ms in it and you've got to leave your comfort zone to taste the plain yellow M&M.

Individuals who aren't willing to be tolerant will stick to eating the plain red M&M all the time. I know how this sort of problem develops. Remember, I'm a psychologist. These individuals have to decide if it's worth working through this problem. I don't necessarily think they'll need eight years of deep, intensive, psychoanalytic therapy to resolve this problem. This is a problem they can pretty much resolve on their own without a therapist.

Remember that friend of mine who likes to eat sushi when she's in town? After I allowed her to enrich my life with sushi, I enjoyed eating sushi. I didn't enjoy being with her during dinner. Okay, so I did enjoy her company, because I only see her once a year. I wonder if I'd enjoy being with her if we didn't eat sushi? I mean, what's sushi got to do with people having good conversation while eating? I'm usually a good conversationalist, so it's easy for anyone I'm eating dinner with to talk to me. I can be funny, serious and, well, that's about it. I really am easy to get along with when I'm taking my medicine regularly. By the way, this friend of mine, she visited this last summer, and I'm aware you don't know which summer I mean. I'm referring to the summer of 2003. My friend has been visiting pretty much every summer, and well, she's all right to be around. That's all I'm going to say about her for now. I do like her a lot, and I miss her during the year. She admitted that she sort of missed me one time four years ago.

Tolerance and How it Affects Others

Now that we've established we need to be intolerant, let's discuss how being tolerant affects those around you. If I accept you, and all of the factors that make you a diverse person, such as your gender, culture and ethnic group, religious affiliation and your sexual orientation, and if I treat you with respect and dignity, then I'm accepting who you want to be. I could resist accepting your right to be who you want to be by insisting that you behave like me. The reason I'd do so is because I prefer familiarity to unfamiliarity. It would be about me wanting you to be like me. My selfish attitude to have you be like me is very self-serving. Self-serving for me, of course, because it's more comforting for me to interact with others who look and talk like me. So, we may become intolerant because of our powerful cultural program. If this applies to you, you are not powerless and you can change. Don't blame me, either, because I've got nothing to do with it. I don't really know you. I'm not saying I wouldn't be interested in knowing you or anything. It's just that I'm pretty much the messenger. I'm trying to teach you how to become tolerant for $13.00, and I think it's a pretty good deal. Well, is there anything wrong? The first sentence of this paragraph should read, "Now that we've established that we need to be tolerant." and not "intolerant." It's another "Yes Captain, I'm Awake" check. Were you asleep or did you catch it? Be honest.

Sociologists theorize that human beings depend on the feedback they receive from others in society to fashion their creative self and stable identity. That's why it's pretty important for human beings to treat each other respectfully. If we don't accept individuals from other cultures by interacting with them in respectful and socially caring ways, then their view of themselves could potentially be unfavorable and negative. You see, human beings interpret the reactions they receive from others about their behavior as either positive or negative.

Why We Need Each Other to Feel Good About Ourselves

The incredibly important thing to remember as you begin your cultural assessment is that all human beings are valuable. You and I have never been, and will not ever be, culturally or personally superior to any other human being. That's pretty much it on this matter.

You also need to realize that all human beings deserve to be treated with respect and dignity; regardless of what country they were born in, their race, culture, how they worship and their life ways. In order for you to experience happiness in your conscious life, as opposed to your dream life, and to feel loved (again in conscious life as opposed to dream life) you need others. You're probably aware that you need others to feel good about yourself. Think about it now. For me to be happy I need other people to satisfy my physical, emotional and spiritual needs. I've got other special needs, but that would require more high-level self-disclosures. Another thing is for you to acknowledge that you and only you, not me, Hank or Herb is responsible for your behavior. No mysterious social force that's following only you around is responsible for your behavior. Your shadow is not responsible for your behavior. You are actually responsible for your shadow's behavior. Ever wonder what a mysterious social force looks like? Lastly, your alter ego is not responsible for your behavior.

The last important thing to remember is that your culture is no better or worse than any other culture. To accept this assertion you have to acknowledge that cultural differences are not bad. Remember the term _cultural relativity?_ It means that what works for one culture may not work for another. It's just that we're so accustomed and culturally programmed to value and reinforce like behavior in our culture. In our culture, there is a phenomenon called **sameness.** It means we all like to behave in similar ways and we value sameness in others. This expectation of sameness is a powerful one to break because, in our society, we are constantly being reinforced for achieving similar things, such as earning exceptional grades, promotions, and other achievements. For example, most Americans lead linear lives. You like that term, linear?

Linear Thinking

Linear comes from the word *line*. Sorry, linear means plotting life events on a line to understand when life-cycle events occur. For example, this view identifies specific events in life, such as when we're supposed to start kindergarten, graduate from high school and college, start a career, get married, have children, begin enjoying gefilte fish and lox, and when to start using topical ointments and an anvil. All of these life-cycle events were observed by researchers studying normal human development. This linear view was developed after researchers studied millions of people like you doing things in life. I know, you're interested in knowing how many subjects in the study used anvils.

The linear view is prescriptive, meaning it shows us how life needs to unfold. I don't need to be told how my life should lay out, because I wrote this book. I'm not necessarily saying you need to be told how your life should unfold. If you're a self-determined, self-directed mature adult exercising your free will, and you know how to inhale, exhale, and evaluate your movement in the natural environment, then you'll do all right. It's just that I don't need to be told what to achieve in my life. Yes, there are other things I need to be told. Again, I'm not going to make any high-level self-disclosures now. Just remember that according to the linear view, life progresses in a certain sequence with life markers.

So what's good about this linear perspective? Well, it certainly does relate to diversity. If everyone in this society is culturally programmed and reinforced for valuing sameness, for achieving the same life-cycle events, then there's less interest in attaining different life-cycle experiences. It just strengthens our convictions that we're doing the culturally right thing if everyone else is doing what we're doing. I'm not saying you shouldn't go to college, not get married or establish job stability because everyone else is doing these life-cycle things. Just be aware of which life experiences you're pursuing, why you're achieving them and what accomplishing them means for you at that time in your wonderful life. Isn't it nice to be innocently following your bliss? We really need to be aware of how often our behavior is influenced by what others are doing. You need to have good self-awareness and be good at self-monitoring. Self-monitoring is just a fancy way of saying I'm awake and aware of what I think, feel, say, and do. Now you know why I test you with my "Yes Captain, I'm Awake" checks. I'm trying to test your self-awareness.

Let's finish tolerance. **Tolerance** means respecting the individuality of each person you interact with in your life. You certainly have the capacity to respect individuals. It means you'll take time to educate yourself about other cultures. Start by asking questions or reading material about other cultures. To understand how other cultures orient themselves to the world, you have to start with understanding their culture-bound values. I really enjoy learning about other cultures and how they orient themselves to the world. I know how I orient myself to the world. Do you know how you orient yourself to your world? Ever wonder how caterpillars orient themselves to their world? I think they'd have to orient themselves to their world twice in their lives. Once as a caterpillar and once as a butterfly. Just an interesting observation, again. Be thankful you only have to orient yourself to the world once in your lifetime. I wonder if the caterpillar's original orientation to its world is similar to the orientation it has as a butterfly?

4

Socialization: So What Do You Want to Know About My Upbringing?

"Children have never been very good at listening to their elders, but they have never failed to imitate them"

—James Baldwin

"Unlike grownups, children have little need to deceive themselves"

—Goethe

"What's done to children, they will do to society"

—Karl Menninger

Let me ask you something. Have you ever heard of the term "***socialization?***" Actually, it's just another one of those fancy, expensive words in my fund of knowledge that I use to impress you. You know what? You've experienced socialization and it accounts in a strong way for who you pretty much are today. If you are a human being who experienced human contact since you began your dash; you know, inhaling, exhaling and interacting with other human beings, then you've undergone socialization. Think about all of the agents that made you who you are today, and consider them as part of a continu-

47

ous journey toward becoming your true, authentic self. You like that? Well, that's socialization. It's about the agents that influenced your development into the undeniably unique, loving, competent, respectful human being that you are. You see, your personality traits were shaped by your socialization experience. You like that word agents?

Agents of Socialization

So, what are agents of socialization? *Agents of socialization* refers to individuals and institutions that shaped your development, such as mom and dad, siblings, peers, school, and the media. These agents are part of the socialization process. Life is one long socialization process. Eating plain brown M&Ms for a lifetime is an incredibly lousy socialization experience. Know what I mean? You never taste red or green M&Ms. This represents a great social injustice and it deprives one of a meaningful enrichment experience.

Primary and Secondary Socialization

Mom and dad raising you is called *primary socialization*. Enlisting in any branch of the armed services represents *secondary socialization.* Attending law school or a police academy are other examples of secondary socialization experiences. You could even call marriage a secondary socialization experience. All I want to say about marriage is that it's an institution pretty much based on romantic love. If you think about how we select our marital partners in Western culture, you'll realize we pretty much choose our mates based on homogamy. *Homogamy* is a fancy word referring to the tendency for people who share similar social characteristics to marry each other. So, when someone asks you why you married your partner, just say we were homogamous at the time we decided to marry, and we're still homogamous. Look, there is such a word as homogamy. It's in the dictionary.

In a marriage, you assume specific, nicely defined roles and the duties assigned to these roles need to be satisfied in order for you to experience marital bliss. That's pretty much all I'll say about marriage. Okay, I'll make a high-level self-disclosure here. I function really well in my roles as a spouse and father. And no, you don't need to ask my spouse to corroborate it. It's about getting socialized into different roles and their duties. I'm in an ***egalitarian marriage,*** meaning there's lots of gender equality, power equality, voice equality, trust, openness, and, well…that's about it. I'm just sorry it took four previous marriages to get this one kind of right.

Now that you know about the agents of socialization, let's discuss how they influenced your development into the wonderful human being that you are today. You know, socialization starts the moment you enter the world. Labor and delivery. Your mom labored and you were delivered to the world. I guess you don't remember much about the joy associated with this experience. I hope your parents remember the joy associated with this experience. Don't feel bad, most people don't remember much about the first day their social life began. Actually, most of us don't recall anything about the first day of our life. Anyway, after everyone welcomes you to our wonderful world, the socialization process steadily begins to unfold.

Socialization refers to the way your mom and dad raised you beginning on day one. I know that healthy socialization begins with mom and dad holding you lots, cuddling you, responding to your needs, such as changing your diapers and feeding you when you got hungry. It's a pretty predictable schedule early on and it's your parent's responsibility to create this safe, trusting, familiar, responsive, and anticipatory-like environment. Oh yeah, your parents also needed to tell you they loved you. Hopefully your parents tell you they love you now. What more validation do you need that you're an intelligent, worthwhile, loved and valued human being?

The Effects of Deprivation and Isolation on Development

The importance of experiencing healthy, optimal early socialization can be seen by the effects of deprivation and isolation on human development. **Deprivation** and **isolation** means little or no human contact. A review of the reported cases of feral children (children reportedly raised by animals) indicates that these children were socially delayed, walking on all four limbs, eating raw food and having no speech. Children who are victims of severe neglect and abuse, such as being confined to closets and hardly fed or bathed are unable to communicate, are fearful and hostile toward others, and are unable to use language to effectively communicate. Sadly, these children suffer emotional, physical, mental, and social disturbances.

Here We Go Again: Nature versus Nurture

The historical debate about what accounts more for influencing human behavior, nature or nurture, reveals that we are products of both influences. **Nature** refers to biological and physiological factors that determine human behavior. Social Darwinists believe an individual's personal characteristics and status in society is determined by their genetic endowment. Behaviorists and social scientists argue that our behaviors are shaped and influenced by everything in our environments. The focus here is on experiences in our natural environment. The **nurture** theory focuses on the effects of social learning and environmental influences on human behavior. Environmental influences include whether you attended private or public school and where you lived. Your family's religious affiliation and its influence on your development of a value and moral system is also an environmental agent responsible for shaping your behavior. Having a father who was an outdoorsman and who taught you to fish and hunt can be considered an environmental influence on your development.

Gordon Allport and his book "The Nature of Prejudice"

Gordon Allport, a famous psychologist, wrote a classic book titled, "The Nature of Prejudice." Allport observed that children are more likely to be tolerant if they are raised in a home where parents are supportive and loving. What do you make of that? Did you ever think there was an association between having supportive, loving parents and a capacity for tolerance in their child? Be honest, no one's going to know except you, and maybe your alter ego.

Parenting is about training children to be capable, responsible, and respectful. Competent parents provide their children with opportunities to make good decisions and they hold them accountable for these decisions. Sounds fair to me. You're probably aware that this isn't a book on competent parenting, fast top fuel cars or neuropsychology. But we've got to discuss competent parenting and its relationship to developing tolerant, respectful, and loving children. What you'll discover is that it's incredibly important for children to experience competent parenting. And yes, I'm a very competent parent who's tolerant, loving, respectful, and just plain well liked by people. I will admit that I don't teach parenting-skills classes.

So, What's a Reasonable-Minded Parent All About?

In general, ***firm, direct, and reasonable-minded parents*** tend to raise healthy, competent children. I'm not referring to domineering, controlling, or coercive parents. I'm describing parents who are competent in many ways—like me. The children of competent parents exercise good self-control, they are socially mature, achieve in school, and they have a healthy self-esteem. Competent parents agree on when and how to set boundaries and limits on their children's behavior in a respectful, warm, and accepting way. These parents lay out reasonable expectations for their children and they explain how their kids can achieve them. Support and encouragement is given to these children. For example, if a child misbehaves, these parents will let their child know they are misbehaving and why their behavior is not acceptable. In addition, they will explain this business in a respectful way without being demeaning. These parents won't totally insult or humiliate their children.

The **competent parent** described here is similar to a competent supervisor. Think about your supervisor at work—and I'm aware I didn't have to say "at work" because that's the only place you probably have a supervisor. I mean, you don't have a supervisor in your marriage, do you? Now, ask yourself if this individual behaves like a competent parent. Does this supervisor treat you with respect, set reasonable performance expectations, counsel you respectfully if you need discipline, and not insult you in the presence of your co-workers? If your supervisor is competent and effective, meaning that he/she cares enough about wanting you to develop your job skills, then you'll likely experience job satisfaction if you like your job. I know, you can have a great supervisor and experience little job satisfaction because you don't like your job. Or you can have a lousy supervisor who interacts with you very little, which is why you experience job satisfaction. In this situation, I suppose you'd have to like your job. Any other combinations here? How about being self-employed and not liking your job? Obviously, you wouldn't have a supervisor to like or not like. What if you were self-employed and were the supervisor who was liked by your employees? Isn't that nice? Okay, enough with the combinations and things. Oh, what if you didn't work?

The Permissive Parent

Other parents who are **permissive** tend to create children who are immature, irresponsible, impulsive, and not motivated to achieve academically. Permissive parents use little control and intervention in their children's lives. Usually, these parents aren't consistent in communicating boundaries and limits to their children's behavior, and if they do, the rules and expectations aren't stated clearly to the children. Consequently, the children interpret their parent's lack of involvement in consequencing their behavior as approval of their behavior. The problem here is the parents don't often create a home environment where mature and responsible behavior is expected of their children.

Allport's Conclusions on the Parenting Styles

Why is it important to study the socialization process and the types of parenting styles that produce healthy and competent children? I'll explain why. Allport learned that children raised by competent parents in loving environments where consistent discipline was practiced and moral guidance and respectful behavior was expected, tended to be more tolerant and less prejudicial. See, that's the connection. As adults they will more likely be flexible minded, empathetic, and compassionate. Children raised in home environments with an absence of consistent discipline, love, lack of moral guidance, and exhibition of how to behave respectfully tend to be intolerant and prejudicial. As adults, they are more likely to be insecure, fearful, distrustful, and self-centered. Imagine being married to someone with these traits. You'd always be accused of eating all the pickles or herring in the house.

Let me share what I've learned working with children, adolescents, and adults since it supports what I have just explained. For the most part, I've concluded that mom and dad have an incredibly important responsibility to raise emotionally healthy and competent children. What do I mean by competent? For me, competency refers to an adequate skill level achieved by your son or daughter. It means your child has acquired sufficient skills, enabling him or her to effectively interact with his or her environment and, most importantly, to solve problems in his or her life. It suggests that your child hasn't just intellectually understood the skills you taught them, but that he or she has mastered and can successfully apply his or her skills. If your child is competent, treat yourself and that other competent adult you live with to a three-year Alaskan land tour and cruise package. If you're a single parent, let me know how much the cruise costs and I'll loan you the money. Trust me here, not about loaning you the money, but about doing a good job parenting and enjoying the benefits of competent parenting. You could be a parent experiencing grief after finding crack cocaine in your 12-year-old's sock and underwear drawer.

How Incompetent Parents Can Perpetuate Prejudicial Attitudes in Their Children

We can admit, with relative confidence, that incompetent parents tend to raise incompetent kids. I'll be careful here and not over generalize. There are some incompetent parents who raise competent children. Not many, though. Has your child ever shared something about his or her friend that concerned you? Maybe while at a friend's home, your child overheard the parents making prejudicial comments about a minority child. You know what I mean here. So, it's reasonable to assume that a parent's prejudicial attitudes can get transmitted to their children. As a parent, it's your responsibility to correct your child's inaccurate cultural assumption, or a prejudice if he or she expresses one. If you neglect to correct it, then you are reinforcing the unfavorable cultural assumption. As a tolerant parent, you'll need to explain why and how human beings tend to make pre-judgments based on limited information, and how that maneuver is the easy way to sum things up about people. Discussing this issue at home with your children conveys to them that it's safe and healthy to discuss the positive aspects of other cultures.

The **media** in this country also plays an important role in the formation of our children's attitudes regarding other cultures. As you know, media includes television, internet, radio and magazines. The tendency is for the media to sometimes portray minority groups in stereotypical roles, which perpetuate negative images of minorities. We need to portray minority group members in positive roles on television and in other media.

How Parents Can Introduce Their Children to Other Racial and Cultural Groups

Remember, parents need to give their children opportunities to interact with children from other cultures. Look for opportunities in your community to expose your kids to children from other cultures. You could start by contacting the YMCA/YWCA, Boys and Girls Clubs, Parks and Recreation programs, after school and weekend programs, and summer camps. Similarly, as parents we should develop friendships with individuals from different racial and cultural groups. To teach children tolerance, parents should introduce games and books that reflect diversity in racial and cultural backgrounds. Parents must explain to their children that it's never permissible to tease other children because of their racial or cultural background.

Here's the Tough Thing You've Got To Do

Being accepting and respecting of an individual from another culture sometimes isn't easy. It means having to tolerate the differences, suspending any early assumptions and pre-judgments your mind makes based on your evaluation of how this individual talks, worships, dresses, and his or her value system. Withholding your pre-judgments until you truly know what this individual is all about will allow him or her to have an equal opportunity to belong, achieve, and contribute to your community. Their community is your community. Imagine a community of people accepting each other without prejudice. It's like a bunch of plain, different colored M&Ms living together in one community. If you haven't figured it out yet, the critical thing to understand here is that children enter the world with the capacity for tolerance. It means they are not born bigoted. The ability to be tolerant is a natural outcome of being raised in a positive, warm, accepting, and loving home environment.

5

Get a Load of This: I Need You, You Need Me and We Need Them

○ ○

"We are born helpless. As soon as we are fully conscious we discover loneliness. We need others physically, emotionally, and intellectually; we need them if we are to know anything, even ourselves"

—*C.S. Lewis*

"I am the inferior of any man whose rights I trample under foot. Men are not superior by reason of the accidents of race and color. They are superior who have the best heart—the best brain. The superior man…stands erect by bending above the fallen. He rises by lifting others"

—*Robert Green Ingersoll*

Let's discuss **acceptance.** Acceptance more than conveys welcome to the club or the neighborhood. If I'm comfortable interacting with you in my club then it expresses my approval of you. For our purposes, we need to discuss how acceptance relates to cultural diversity. Remember, if you look like me, dress like me, and talk like me, then I'll be more likely to accept you. However, if you don't, I'll be less likely to accept you based on some differences that shows your otherness, such as your physical features.

Self-Acceptance and Self-Esteem

Before we discuss acceptance of others, we need to examine *self-accep-tance,* you know, accepting yourself for who you are and what you're all about. Can you imagine that? We've got to start with you again, at the individual level of analysis. It's just a fancy way of saying it all starts with you. By the way, you need to consider if accepting yourself means you accept your alter ego. It does. You know yourself pretty well, so start by asking yourself if you've got high self-esteem. Not high triglycerides. I sure hope you have high self-esteem. If you do, then it's more likely you'll let others know how you feel and think about things. *Self-esteem*, as it relates to culture, enables you to perceive yourself and others as important and valuable people. You won't be uncomfortable sharing with others how you feel about them, and you'll be interested in pursuing lasting and meaningful relationships with people. I suspect that you'll also feel equal to others; meaning you won't feel culturally or personally superior or inferior to others. Even if you perceive differences in abilities, you won't attribute the differences to race. This means you're a mature individual. For example, you'll know that your ability to swim faster than the other swimmer has nothing to do with your race. It's got everything to do with you learning to swim when you were two years old and because you're a triathlete. Period.

"Otherness" and Social Marginality

Think about the M&M situation. If all of the M&Ms in the bag were plain brown M&Ms, it would be boring in that bag. If they could talk to each other, they would probably express their acceptance of each other. However, if you introduced a plain green M&M into the bag of plain brown M&Ms, things would change. A phenomenon called *"Otherness"* would occur in the bag of M&Ms. All of the plain brown

M&Ms would discover there was a plain green M&M in their community, and they have never seen or interacted with a plain green M&M. It would create lots of anxiety and concern in their community. If they could talk, they would start talking about the plain green M&M, asking themselves where this M&M came from and what this different looking M&M's agenda was all about. Everyone has an agenda. Lots of anxiety, fear, and curiosity would surface in the community of plain brown M&Ms. The brown M&Ms would suspect that the green M&M was a spy.

So, the green M&M will experience social marginality because it wasn't accepted and integrated into the community of plain brown M&Ms. This phenomenon called *social marginality* is the outcome of a diverse situation where someone feels excluded from the dominant community. As a result, our green M&M feels rejected. This poor, plain green M&M will live with the distressing awareness of being an outsider, and not enjoying the social advantages that all the other brown M&Ms have in their community. Sadly enough, this situation illustrates how social diversity can be divisive in society. It shows how a group of plain brown M&Ms can affect the life of a green M&M.

After some time, I suppose, the plain brown M&Ms would notice that the only difference between them and the plain green M&M is their color. I'd assume that after the plain brown M&Ms interacted and developed meaningful relationships with the plain green M&M, they'd learn that they share many cultural characteristics, such as speaking the same language and having the same social, psychological and physical needs. The brown M&Ms would probably conclude that they felt comfortable interacting with the plain green M&M because they had learned this M&M was just like them on the inside.

Once the brown M&Ms discover they like the green M&M, they will have learned more about themselves in the process. I believe we can know ourselves better by studying others. You don't have to agree with me here, but think about it. Observing and studying others allows us to see how others are similar to and different from us. The value is in using this information to increase our awareness as to why we experience anxiety when we are around others who look different or speak another language. To achieve this, though, you need to be conscious of the reaction you have to seeing the plain green M &M. You actually need to be good at self-monitoring.

Race

Let's discuss *race.* Racial characteristics are the most obvious features about you and me. It's what you observe about me first when I decide to sit next to you on the train. I'm thinking you'll notice the color of my skin first and what I'm wearing. What else is there to notice about me? Beyond the physical features, ambiguous and uncertain stuff is what your mind doesn't necessarily want to deal with when I sat next to you. So, what does your mind do with the ambiguous stuff? It fabricates material that is acceptable to you, so you can reach some conclusion about what to do with me sitting next to you. It's a strategy. You may determine you can't tolerate sitting next to me, even though I haven't said a word to you. You may just get up and move to another seat. Imagine if I attempted to start a conversation with you.

The Importance of Belonging

Everybody has a need to *belong*; to simply and innocently belong. It was John Donne who said, "No man is an island, entire of itself." All human beings have a need to belong. I think belongingness is biologically based, meaning we have an instinct to belong to groups. The reason it's so important is because it gives us recognition, security, an identity, and, I suppose, friendship. I feel incomplete as a human being if I don't belong to something or other. Belonging is also about being a part of a larger community of people who acknowledge, accept, and respect you and your contributions to their group. I'm always trying to be accepting and inclusionary. I just wish everybody else was accepting and inclusionary of me.

We can start by agreeing we all belong to our society. You want to reduce it further? All right, you belong to your family of origin. Look, I want to belong. I belong to my immediate family and my kids belong to me. I'd like them to move out, but they're too young to move out at 16 and 13. My spouse and I belong to each other. No, I don't want my spouse to move out, despite her being clearly capable of pursuing a self-directed, self-determined, very independent life. I want my spouse to continue living with me in this sort of conjugal, loving, and meaningful living arrangement, with a very semi-independent living arrangement for the 16 and 13 year old. I know, I didn't need to say sort of conjugal. It either is or isn't conjugal. It would be awfully nice if my kids volunteered to move out, and I'd help with the rent. They could move around the corner and go to the same school. And no, my wife doesn't want me to move out. She likes me lots.

Do me a favor and think about the different groups you belong to. If you work, you belong to your work group, department, or the organization. If you're a college student you belong to the undergraduate or graduate club. And if you've got a circle of friends, you belong to this group. I'm sure you belong to a few groups. It's pretty much a given you belong to many groups. My house will belong to me after I pay off the mortgage and turn 96. ***Belonging*** usually begins with your immediate family, followed by your extended family, and ending with your community, state, country and well, let' see now, your world. One day I'll belong to that community who has left us for eternity.

We don't have to discuss this further. It's just a reminder of our mortality. Don't let the dreadful death anxiety get to you, now. I'm over the dread, because I've pretty much accepted that I will die one day. It took me 24 years to work through this death anxiety. I remember experiencing unforgiving psychic pain knowing my existence was time limited. I became fully aware that my existence was temporal; that I couldn't make a deal with G-d or anything like that. It was the great existential philosopher Kierkegaard who put it so nicely when he proclaimed that my conflict is simply about wanting a finite existence and knowing, again, in an agonizing way, that I'll die one day. That's about it on this subject now. I've got no lousy choice except to work through the miserable anxiety, anguish, agony, angst, and well, dread again.

How did we derail and land on existentialism? I don't know about you, but existentialism has a tendency to leave you feeling pretty hopeless, at least that's what it does to me. Is that what it does to you? Why should we keep focusing on how man's awareness of his existence in a temporal world results in his ruminating over inescapable death? It only leads us to experience more anguish, grief, and futility. Look, death is inevitable and I suppose nothingness follows our death. Well, I don't know that for sure. How much more nothingness can I experience when I'm dead? And how do I know I *can* experience nothingness when I'm dead? Can you experience anything when you're dead? I wonder if my alter ego dies when I die? How do you know for sure that while you're alive you're truly experiencing things? Maybe it's just an incredible grand illusion, this thing called "consciousness." What do you think? I guess I won't know until I cross over to the other side. Who knows, maybe everyone on the other side is doing all of the experiencing, while we just think we're experiencing life. It's pretty confusing isn't it? If I see you on the other side, we'll pick this conversation up and finish it.

Belonging to Groups

Let's discuss groups. Groups didn't accidentally surface one day in our culture for no reason. The phenomenon of groups resulted from our desire to join others interested in achieving a common goal. How's that sound? Human beings probably realized they couldn't achieve certain personal goals by themselves. So, groups were created to allow individual group members to pursue interdependent goals and to satisfy individual needs. Example: This club I'm a member of motivates me to train and stay fit for life. There is a lot of mutual influence in the group, too. I strongly believe that each of us in the group influences each other in a positive way. Each of us affects each other in desired ways, motivating each other to show up for the swim and run program Monday through Friday. We hold each other accountable to train each morning. It's called *interpersonal influence.*

We need to now discuss *group norms.* All groups have norms to guide the behavior of the group members. Norms are the policies and rules agreed to by group members to facilitate acceptable behavior and the desired attitude of members in the group. The agreed upon norms of the group function to maintain *internal consistency,* such as consistent behavior among group members. Norms help group members better predict and anticipate how other members will behave.

The Fit For Life Club Because It Can't Be Living For Fitness Club

Let me tell you about an informal fitness club I belong to. I'm one of five members in this club and all of us live three to four houses from each other. We run, lift weights, and swim. I've been trying to convince the other guys to cycle so we could become a triathlon club. I like cycling, and I've got a triathlon bike that I purchased a few years ago. In other words, I'm the only triathlete and I've been doing triathlons for about seven years now.

My buddies and I run on Tuesday and Thursday mornings at 5:30 a.m. On Sundays, we'll either plan to run together or run alone. We'll run between four and six miles on the run days. For the last couple of years we've been swimming on Monday, Wednesday and Friday at 5:30 a.m. at an outdoor olympic-size pool. We swim for about an hour and cover pretty much a mile or more worth of laps and since money isn't involved here, you need to trust me on this. My partners think I cheat when it comes to counting laps. Trust me, I don't cheat counting laps. Anyway, enough about swimming. It's got absolutely nothing to do with cultural diversity or tolerance. Well, actually it does. I have to tolerate them accusing me of being dishonest.

Two of the guys I run with have been running together for about 18 years. I moved into the neighborhood about eight years ago, around 1996, and started running with them six years ago. I'm the youngest member in the club. One of the founding members has been trying to get me to pay membership dues since I joined the club. I've never paid membership dues or completed a membership application because there isn't one. He's trying to make me feel socially marginal because I'm not paying membership dues. I know I'm socially integrated into this club because none of the members have insisted that I resign from the club. I also know that none of the other members pay membership dues. What do you think? I just don't trust this founding member. I have no idea what they'd spend the dues on for the club members. There's absolutely nothing any of the members receive for being members of this exclusive club of like consciousness. We're just ordinary club members with ordinary privileges. Nothing fancy at all.

If one member of the group refuses to honor the group norms, problems will develop. In our club, if one member slacks and doesn't show for the morning swim or run program, he'll be labeled a slacker. This is an example of a group member not internalizing the norms of the group. You won't get teased if you're sick or something. It's each group member's responsibility to consistently enforce the group's norms. It's really all about conforming to the norms of the group, which is good practice for conforming to society's norms. People who don't conform to society's norms are nonconformists and are likely to experience trouble with the law.

I suspect the founding member created this club because he had a strong need to belong to, you know, a group of men sharing a like consciousness. He'll undoubtedly deny it. The club allows me to affiliate and identify with a special brotherhood or in-group. I get a spiritual infusion of this life force, which feeds directly into my unobstructed artery. I suppose it's also the meaningful intergroup interaction that's so fulfilling for me. Sadly enough, I can't get any of the other members to articulate, in a meaningful way, why they're in the club and what it does for them emotionally and spiritually. I've quit asking because they told me I aggravate them too much with my ridiculous questions. So, I was told to drop the questions or I'd be dropped from the club. I decided to drop the questions. I was just trying to get them to more deeply articulate what being around a brotherhood of men at 5:30 in the morning means. I asked them if they felt they mattered to the other members of the club, and if the club nourished their sense of self. I also asked them if they valued the close attachments and intimacy they developed toward each other and if the club added meaning and purpose to their life. Sadly enough, a couple of them commented that I was the only one who didn't matter to them and that they didn't value anything in the club. I ended up creating a diagnosis for all of them, "Male Intimacy Anxiety Disorder."

I'll tell you what I think. I know that all four of them have a need to belong and to express their desire for intimacy and affectional attachments. They will deny it, but they have a need to exchange warm, close communication with each other. I sure do. I will admit, though, I feel that I need them emotionally much more than they need me emotionally. And no, I'm not overly dependent on any of them for anything else. I've got a meaningful and purposeful life outside of the club. Remember, I'm married and have two kids.

What Running Means and What it Discloses About Others

What do you know about running? I'm not suggesting you need to know a lot about running. Running is grueling. Exclamation Point. It reveals your vulnerabilities, like what's inside of you and how you respond to physical and psychological challenges. Running exposes the true you and not the fake you. I mean, when you run, you pretty much can't fake running fast, and why would you fake running slow? If you run slowly it's because your legs move slow. So, if you want to know somebody quickly, just invite him or her for a three-mile run on a Sunday morning. You don't need to spend money on dinner and a movie.

You'll leave the running experience knowing everything about the individual, and be able to decide if you want to see him or her again. You'll spend about $1.25 on a 16 oz. bottle of Gatorade, and another $1.50 on a good powerbar. Let's see, that's a total of $2.75. See; compare that to about $60 for dinner and a movie. Have you ever experienced psychic pain putting out $60 on a date, and knowing with absolute certainty that you'll never see that nice, well-meaning, but poorly matched-to-you human being again? Just something to think about.

Vulnerability means wearing shorts when it's about 40 degrees at 5:30 in the morning. I know, you could wear long sweat pants. If you wear running shorts, we see your skinny, bony legs. If you wear long sweat pants, you're hiding your skinny, bony legs. Vulnerability is resisting incredibly powerful, highly persuasive, intrusive thoughts of slowing down around mile one of your six-mile run, or quitting the lousy run altogether. It means getting beat on some days. This presents no problem if you run alone. The problem, however, is that you are not running alone.

Think about running. The pounding your joints absorb is brutal. Ever notice that runners who race say belonging to a club inspired them to train regularly? You see, the club is the anchor that strengthens their will and drive to train. That's a testimony to the power of belonging. Knowing that you belong to a club sustains your motivation to train. Think about it. So what does this group do for me? It's sort of an in-group keeping me strongly committed to staying fit. At times, I think of the club as a social group of men united, and proud, who enjoy spending time together getting fit. We've developed close, personal relationships that are mutually fulfilling. Well, at least I think so. I think the group represents aging men sharing a sort of "consciousness of like despair" as we age and manage physical decline. I mean, that's pretty much why we're staying fit. It's absolutely about delaying death. I suppose it's also about lowering our risk of coronary artery disease.

It's not a race against time, a downhill slide or drift into an abyss of inescapable anguish. Now for the bad news. Just kidding. Don't worry,

I'm not derailing into existentialism. That's all. Oh sure, there are values and loyalties we have to each other and the group that strengthens cohesion. And no, I don't slack a whole lot. Don't confuse me with someone else you know that's a slacker. Remember, you're always a member of some kind of team. The team you belong to needs you, you need them, and well, there's a larger team out there that needs your team. I'm not sure if you need your alter ego. Your alter ego probably needs you. Maybe there's a group your alter ego can belong to. I'll get back to you on that later.

6

"That's Pretty Much the Way It Is Around Here Pal"

o o o o o o o o o o o o o o o o o o o o o o o o o o o o

"In the everyday world, one is under the strongest compulsion to construe things one way or another"

—*Walker Percy*

"It is a little bit embarrassing to have been concerned with the human problem all one's life and find at the end that one has no more to offer by way of advice than try to be a little kinder"

—*Aldous Huxley*

Civilization is the order and freedom promoting cultural activity"

—*Will Durant*

Is what I see around here the way it's supposed to be? I think so. I mean, I have an ideal image of society. My ideal image of how things ought to be around here is different from the way things really are. It's all about the gap. There's a gap between how I want things to be and the way things really are. It's a pretty wide gap. I need to work on shrinking the gap because society isn't going to shrink the gap for me. Society will not undergo social change for you or me. You and I pretty much have to do the changing. Period. Look, it's not so bad. You and I adjust to changing social conditions all the time. Otherwise, we'd experience more problems in living. Problems in living can mean trouble with the law, not establishing job stability, marital discord or having to visit pawnshops.

I guess you need to know where around here is. Around here is contemporary, mainstream America. It's what you see when you look outside and survey modern times. Around here is where I live, the United States of America. More specifically, I live in Southern California. I'm not pretentious or anything, so I won't reveal what exclusive, sort-of beach community and, well, naturally, highly desirable area I live in. It's just not important. There are lots of highly preferred communities for entrepreneurial types like me to live in within Southern California. Revealing where I live will only create a wider gap between your social class and mine. Listen, I still interact with a broad class of people, some of whom, understandably so, are hangers on. All right, I'm not really an entrepreneur and I don't live in an affluent beach community or on the bluff. I do, however, enjoy occupational prestige.

In this chapter, we'll discuss current social problems such as social inequality, social differentiation, and exclusion. I'll also discuss how language originated. Language has the potential to be a social problem. It can pretty much start a fight, and I'd consider a fight to be a social problem. I'm talking about a fight where somebody ends up needing a couple of bandages, some ice and lots of unconditional tender, loving care.

Language

Let's start with language. Everyone needs to use **language** to have his or her needs met in any society. A culture could not survive without language. Think of language as a set of symbols with shared meanings. It's a method human beings use to communicate with each other. If you want me to get you some Ben and Jerry's ice cream, a bandage or some topical ointment, you need to express that to me. Ben and Jerry's is wonderful ice cream, you know, gourmet stuff that costs about $3.99 a pint. If I really like you, I'll get you a pint. Otherwise, sorry. So, what's the point here, besides Ben and Jerry's being great ice cream? Human beings are able to assign objects like ice cream and different topical ointments with meaning through the use of language.

You and I assign meaning to a bunch of things. For starters, you probably don't assign much meaning to my Ph.D., do you? I think you should assign it a lot of meaning. But that's my feeling and I shouldn't talk for you or expect you to assign my Ph.D. lots of meaning. Look, if you had a Ph.D. I'd assign it lots of meaning, and I'd pretty much be happy for you. You may assign lots of meaning to a favorite drill bit or a stent. A stent is a device made of stainless steel that's inserted into an artery that's occluded. Human beings assign meaning to all sorts of objects and experiences so we can communicate. In the end, humans living in this symbolic environment create social order and a culture. Here's the thing, though. Sometimes subjective interpretations can be asserted like Starbuck's ice cream being better than Ben and Jerry's. You're wrong here if you make this statement. But again, at least I have a language to tell you you're wrong. Ben and Jerry's is the best ice cream. Or you might feel that your favorite thrift store has better bargains than mine.

In our society, things like class, gender, and status often influence one's use of language. Also, ask yourself if language influences the development of culture. Benjamin Lee Whorf postulated that language is a shaping force that permeates all aspects of a culture, and enables members of a society to express themselves in certain, habitual ways that guide our thoughts and behavior. Do you like the name Whorf? Imagine how he felt.

It really doesn't matter which language develops in a society as long as everyone speaks the same language. If everyone agrees to speak the same language, then we can communicate and function in our society. Can we agree that social life is a requirement for our survival? If you agree, then social life also enables human beings to get as much of their needs and desires satisfied. Social life is pretty much a cooperative activity humans engage in to sustain their civilization. A fancier term to express social life is psychosocial interaction. You like that? Yes, psychosocial.

I suspect that, for most of the time, people understand each other because they speak the same language and honor the same norms. I know, I said most of the time. Unfortunately, when people are unconventional in behavior it's usually not due to misunderstanding the language of others. It's because of other reasons. It's the blatant violation or refusal to obey rules that gets them into trouble with the law.

Let me sum up by saying that our language guides our thinking and creates consistent and predictable patterns of behavior. If I say I'll pick you up at 6:30 to go to dinner, then you'll expect me at 6:30. If I ask you to please loan me your favorite hammer, I hope you'd let me borrow it and trust that I'll return it to you. Or, if I tell you that I'll get you some fresh bagels, and I end up buying you the four-day-old bagels that are heavily discounted, you'd be angry with me. I wouldn't do that, though, unless you've been aggravating me.

What else does language do for us? Think about how your socioeconomic status (low, middle or high) influences your language and world view. Look at me for example. I'm clearly in the high-socioeconomic status category with my Ph.D. I'm not sure where you are. I don't want to appear arrogant, but you know what I drive. Being in the high-socioeconomic status will probably influence where I'll live, the friends I associate with, what I'll do with my friends, and the kinds of things I'll purchase. I'll probably buy expensive things, like my Vanagon. Do you ever listen to how high-socioeconomic status people talk and what they talk about?

The Language of High Society

I'll try not to stereotype too much here, but some; okay, less than some of these people have a certain view that tends to reflect and be consistent with a high society lifestyle. You see, there is a look that people living in high society reveal to others. Let's consider these people as living in their own subculture. And no, I wasn't giving you a "Yes Captain,

I'm Awake" check by writing that my limited edition, Wolfsburg Vanagon is a class-act car owned by individuals in the high-socioeconomic status category. It is. Period.

Although some of these people feel special and deserving of preferential treatment, they still have to wait in line at the market. So, some high-class people like to establish and preserve class and status distinctions for themselves. Know what I mean? It's about looking and feeling important by displaying status and expensive things. Ever try to get into a very exclusive, affluent private community on the bluffs overlooking the Pacific? I can't even penetrate that neighborhood. There's a gate and you need the code to get in. My theory about why these people erect walls around themselves is to remind me I'm not like them. I'm not special. Would you get a load of that, me not being special?

Remember discussing *"otherness?"* I represent "otherness," which is other than their social class ranking. High-class people interact with each other in their high-class communities. For example, imagine Donald Trump jumping into a public pool at the local recreation center. For sure, he'd complain about the murky water and stuff, and feel all too crowded in that public pool with all the ordinary public Hanks. I'll admit my assumptions may not apply to all high-class people living in these communities. Sadly enough, some blatantly assert being personally superior to me. Remember, the worth and measure of an individual is in his heart and not in his $200 shirt.

How We Treat Money in Our Culture

I'm feeling philosophical right now. My all-time favorite social theorist, Ernest Becker, wrote about money and how human beings treat it in modern society. Becker summarizes Norman Brown's historical definition of *money* as representing a sacred, magical object human beings relish as their gateway to immortality. Becker basically believes that human beings assign great value to things that give life, that enable them to overcome what ordinary people cannot overcome. For Becker, money is sacred because it grants some power over others. Think about it: Money, like a lot of it, gives people freedom from responsibilities of caring for their home, parents, children, car and other things. More importantly, and, in a powerful and visible way, money separates the ordinary, routine life of Hank from the perversely wealthy Lance. Money makes Lance look quite different from Hank. Money enables Lance to distance his likeness to Hank.

Becker, in agreeing with Brown, asserts that money gives human beings a limitless ability to indulge in their every passion, especially material items. The connections both of these theorists make is the one between money, sacredness and power. So, for Becker, power is the medium man uses to deny his mortality. Lots of money can pretty much keep me alive longer than it can you if you've got less of it. Becker puts it like this:

> "Power means power to increase oneself, to change one's natural situation from one of smallness, helplessness, finitude, to one of bigness, control, durability, importance. In its power to manipulate physical and social reality money in some ways secures one against contingency and accident; it buys bodyguards, bulletproof glass, and better medical care. Most of all, it can be accumulated and passed on, and so radiates its powers even after one's death, giving one a semblance of immortality as he lives in the vicarious enjoyment of his heirs that his money continues to buy, or in the magnificence of the art works that he commissioned, or in the statues of himself and the majesty of his own mausoleum. In short, money is the human mode par excellence of coolly denying animal boundness, the determinism of nature."

In talking about the items money can furnish for us, Becker writes that the house, car, and bank account represent one's immortality symbols. I agree with Becker that immortality symbols, like all of the visible physical items, and their worth, are the only things one has to grant one's eternal life. I also think it's just so pathetic. In the following passage Becker notes under what conditions one feels his or her immortality or significance in the world is threatened:

"Or, put another way, if a Black man moves next door, it is not merely that your house diminishes in real estate value, but that you diminish in fullness on the level of visible immortality—and so you die".

Sadly enough, in sum, Becker concluded that human beings transformed from a social animal that gave and passed on to one that was principally interested in amassing and keeping things. The historical taking of objects and falsely believing that this motive represents self-determination and self-direction in life, and by calculating interest on money earned in the bank, one bought into the illusion that one was in total and absolute control of one's destiny.

Social Differentiation and Social Class

Let's discuss social differentiation. ***Social differentiation*** refers to how people differ across certain variables. It's about how we define and distinguish between categories, such as age, gender and race, which are pretty objective. However, it gets more subjective when we try to assign individuals to categories such as socioeconomic class and political affiliation. For example, after taking a good look at me, you'd assign me to the high-status and high-occupational-prestige category. Period. What you'll notice about me is that I embody what professionalism and maturity is all about.

What about ***social class***? I think it's difficult trying to assign someone to a social class. I just know that about three to five percent of the people living in the United States are in the upper class. About 40 to 50 percent are in the middle class, 30 to 40 percent in the working class and 15 to 20 percent in the lower socioeconomic class. I'm in the upper class because of the car I drive. How do you determine what social class you belong to? Sociologists believe that social stratification arose after observing that human beings can be ranked according to many levels. Sadly enough, in contemporary society human beings are unequal due to genetic and environmental factors influencing our development. Some of us end up receiving unequal treatment when it comes to enjoying social privileges.

I believe some human beings have an insatiable desire for things, and I think, regardless of how much human beings possess, some always want more. My explanation for this behavior is that these valued objects have enduring status value. Individuals who obtain status symbols like to keep them, and desire to continue inheriting big, fancy expensive items that display their social status. Thus, our system of **stratification** evaluates people on factors such as wealth, power and prestige. You know, social class is synonymous with socioeconomic status. I've included a brief description of each of these factors.

Wealth

In our Western society, we generally rank people with money and material possessions higher on the scale. These possessions include their impressive homes, the community they live in, number and kinds of cars, their expensive clothes, watches and jewelry. Value is placed on wealth and expensive possessions and the people owning these expensive materials need you to know it so you can admire them and their possessions. The term status symbol was created to describe these items. The thing is, you may not ever meet these individuals, so they will simply display their social class to you by what they drive or where they live.

Power

Individuals can also be ranked according to how much power they possess. Power is the ability of one individual or group to impact or change the behavior of another individual or group. Not surprisingly, power is often associated with wealth, which means that wealthy people have power. You pretty much knew that, though, didn't you? The important thing to know, however, is that power is not distributed equally in society. Only a few people in our society have power.

Prestige

What do you think prestige refers to? What is and isn't prestige is subjectively determined and refers to an individual who enjoys a special distinction or reputation in society. It may mean prestige in occupation—such as certain occupations having high prestige compared to occupations with low prestige. Occupations with high prestige include being a Supreme Court justice, physician, college professor, and well, lawyers. Occupations with low prestige are shoe shiners, garbage collectors, janitors, and security workers. Let me remind you that I didn't create this list of occupational prestige. It actually comes from a study, conducted by Robert Hodge, Donald Treiman, and Peter Rossi (1966), which ranked occupations according to prestige. These researchers ranked occupations based on prestige scores assigned to them by Americans like you and me. They first surveyed Americans in 1947, but through the years, the scores have consistently remained the same. Not surprisingly Americans were most impressed with occupations that required professional skills, political power, and high incomes.

Occupational Prestige Ratings in the United States:

Occupation	Prestige Score
U.S. Supreme Court Justice	94
Physician	93
Nuclear Physicist	92
Scientist	92
State Governor	91
Cabinet Member in Federal Government	90
College professor	90
U.S. Representative in Congress	90
Lawyer	89
Diplomat in U.S. Foreign Service	89
Dentist	88
Architect	88
Psychologist	87
Minister	87
Mayor of a Large City	87
Priest	86
Civil Engineer	86
Airline Pilot	86
Banker	85
Biologist	85
Sociologist	83
Instructor in Public School	82
Accountant in a Large Business	81
Building Contractor	80
Musician in a Symphony Orchestra	78

Occupation	Prestige Score
Author of Novels	78
Economist	78
Electrician	76
Undertaker	74
Police Officer	72
Radio Announcer	70
Bookkeeper	70
Insurance Agent	69
Carpenter	68
Mail Carrier	66
Plumber	65
Barber	63
Garage Mechanic	62
Truck Driver	59
Clerk in a Store	56
Taxi Driver	49
Janitor	48
Bartender	48
Garbage Collector	39

Did you notice where I was ranked on the table of occupational prestige? I'm a psychologist and a college professor. As a psychologist, I get a score of 87 and, as a college professor I get a score of 90. Now, I do not need to feel important, but it's awful nice knowing people in this society assign psychologists and college professors' high prestige scores. Again, it means I enjoy a special distinction in society. Let me tell you something, I think I should enjoy special recognition in society. I mean, I'm not always getting the unconditional respect I deserve.

The unfortunate, unavoidable reality is that social differentiation leads to *social inequality*. Remember the categories that were created based on personal, biological and physical differences? Well, individuals in society created a ranking system to classify these differences. The problem, however, with this ranking system is in the social meaning individuals assign to the ranked characteristics. What worries me is what we do with the social meaning associated with being African-American, Asian, and Hispanic, affluent or living in poverty, young or old. I know about these social meanings and the effects they have on individuals being ranked. Imagine people's race determining where they are ranked in the system. It sounds unfair to me. The assumption one makes when ranking others based on race is that an individual's behavior is determined by their physical characteristics.

Do me a favor right now (as opposed to six years from now) and ask yourself this question: "What accounts for social differentiation in our society?" Don't worry, this isn't a "Yes Captain, I'm Awake" check. Think about whether our innate makeup accounts for the observed differences in abilities between human beings. In other words, we begin with exploring whether an individual's innate abilities, such as being intelligent or a really good problem solver, enable him or her to lead a more satisfying life. The competing theory suggests that social differentiation and social inequality isn't a result of an individuals innate makeup, but rather a function of how he/she is affected by institutions in society. For example, according to structural theory, social differentiation and social inequality results from how our society is structured or how some institutions function. *Structural explanations* for why social inequality occurs may be related to how capitalism operates as an economic system resulting in unequal education, blocked access to resources or other problems related to social and economic conditions. So, political and economic factors may account for the pervasive patterns that sustain social inequality and institutional forms of discrimination against minorities. The problem now is how some institutions may be serving individuals differentially.

Cultures exist because people are interested in getting their social, psychological, spiritual, and physical needs met. It's about a group of people making sincere commitments to cooperate with each other in a social setting. I've pretty much concluded that for a culture to survive, its members must establish the institution of marriage and religion. The rules and norms guiding acceptable and unacceptable behavior need to be enforced through some institution, such as law enforcement, the judicial system and the penal system. See, there needs to be institutions in society to guide conformity and obedience.

Cultural Competence

What about cultural competence? You can probably define **cultural competence** yourself. It's about being competent enough to interact respectfully with a culture. It means acknowledging and respecting ethnic and religious differences, races, socioeconomic classes of individuals, and interacting effectively with these different people. I know that by respecting the different ways people think about things, I convey acceptance, and it makes it easier to interact with people from different cultures. Look, sometimes we should ask more out of ourselves, which means doing more than just good enough.

If we deepen our definition of cultural competence, we integrate knowledge of a certain culture into our ordinary ways of interacting. Remember, culture is defined as patterns of behavior by a group of people. It's their shared characteristics, such as thoughts, symbolic communication system, behavior, customs, values, beliefs, myths, and religion. For you to brag about being culturally competent, you need to weave in and out of other cultures without being insulting. Yes, without offending individuals in a culture by making insensitive, disrespectful comments about their behavior. If you want to be culturally competent, learn all you can about a culture and interact with the members of that culture in respectful ways and be culturally savvy.

Cultural Self-Assessment

I think the only thing left to say about cultural competence is being aware of your cultural assumptions. To be aware of your cultural assumptions, you need to have the courage to do a **cultural-self assessment.** A cultural self-assessment is a self-examination exercise. It's like getting out from behind your eyes and observing how you interact, think, and feel around other cultures. Assess yourself for cultural tension, search for your degree of openness and acceptance when you're interacting with other cultures. If you truly value diversity, you'll challenge yourself to view otherness as an opportunity to understand and strengthen your cross-cultural competence.

It's not easy doing a cultural self-assessment. You probably don't think you need self-evaluating. Imagine doing a cultural self-assessment and ending up with a pretty dispassionate view of yourself. The purpose of doing a cultural self-assessment is to determine if you need to reformulate, modify or redefine your view of other cultures. If you decide to think and feel differently about individuals from other cultures, you'll have to redefine and reconstruct your deeply internalized images, thoughts, and feelings about individuals. You'll have to change your strategies for interacting with individuals from other cultures and transition to feeling comfortable with your new patterns of social interaction. Once you reach this stage of bias-free communication with people from other cultures, you can proudly assert you're a culturally competent and self-aware human being.

Look, we know that not everyone has the capacity or desire to do a cultural self-assessment. Try asking a Neo-Nazi or member of the Ku Klux Klan to do a cultural self-assessment to identify and remove their racial or cultural biases about others. They'd have to be introspective and raise their awareness to new levels. I know these hate groups would admit they're fully aware of who they like and don't like, and are able to justify their reasons. There's no need for them to do a cultural self-assessment. These groups hate Jews, African Americans, individuals with different sexual orientations and different religious beliefs. So, a hate group is any organization whose mission is to promote hostility and hate against people belonging to a specific racial, religious, or cultural group.

Ethnocentrism

Now let's discuss **ethnocentrism.** It's another fancy word in my fund of knowledge. Ethnocentric individuals make blatant assertions of personal and cultural superiority; believing that their race, faith and way of life is the right and best way. The right way of living is their culture's way and the ethnocentric individual enjoys a sense of self-glorification. If I were ethnocentric, I'd profess that my race or culture is better than yours. One reason I'd say my culture is better than yours is because it strengthens my group solidarity. It makes me feel special and valued as a member of my preferred culture. The ethnocentric polarity can have destructive consequences. After my culture identifies your culture as an unfriendly neighbor, we could harm or conquer your culture. It would represent a legitimate reason for war or conflict. So, ethnocentric individuals over identify with the moral and ethical rightness of their culture, which only inhibits their opportunities for change and incorporating other culture-bound value systems into their closed culture.

The problem with the ethnocentric position is that no culture is right or wrong; superior or inferior to any other. It's not about my culture being better than yours. Cultures will always be different from each other. For example, earlier we discussed individualist and collectivist cultures. These are just fancy terms to describe whether cultures focus on the individual or the community. **Individualist cultures** emphasize the value of the individual and **collectivist cultures** focus on the value of the group or society rather than the individual.

Ethnocentrism is bad. It strengthens membership in a culture and enables members to experience a sense of belonging. It is, however exclusionary to others who look, talk and behave differently. All of us need to belong to a certain group. We talked about that earlier. By feeling anchored and strongly attached to your culture, you become emotionally and intellectually invested, and you're willing to give economically, politically, and physically to contribute to the survival of your culture. The difficult thing here for the ethnocentric individual is to continue feeling strongly bonded to his or her own culture and not threatened by other cultures. The ethnocentric individual needs to appreciate other cultures and different ways of living. The goal for ethnocentric individuals should be to understand and appreciate how other cultures choose to live, but they don't necessarily need to approve it.

Remember, beginning at birth we identify with powerful role models, such as our parents who are responsible for socializing and training us to be competent, tolerant and happy children. The socialization process includes believing that our theories, cultural assumptions and life ways are right. So, we accept as truth our assumptions about our cultural norms and values, and we resist looking at and appreciating the life ways of other cultures. Any culture that perceives itself as morally and culturally superior to other cultures is ethnocentric. In the end, ethnocentric individuals act on their impulses to divide the world into two parts. The result is an "Us and Them" perspective.

The "Us" and Them" Perspective

The *"Us and Them" view* is an oversimplification of how members composing the "Them" culture behave. For example, individuals of one culture have assumptions about why other cultures worship the way they do, why they have their particular form of government and economy, how they think about life, and what they do to lead satisfying lives. The problem, however, lies in how our assumptions tend to mislead us. Look, I know assumptions are necessary, but as it relates to culture, assumptions result in restrictive thinking, meaning that they limit further thinking. Thus, a bunch of inaccurate assumptions can lead to faulty thinking about a group of people in a culture. Just think about how our culture and how your socialization program reinforced you to trust that your culture, its values and life ways was the right way.

Remember when we discussed why we need to have the courage to do a cultural self-assessment? We need to truly expose our assumptions to factual accounts of how other cultures behave and if necessary, modify our cultural assumptions to reflect what we've learned. We have to honestly ask ourselves why we hold certain assumptions about things. If we can't engage in this self-examination process to reveal our inaccurate assumptions, we will continue to be anchored to our cognitively constricted, narrow minded view of things. How do you like that language? Cognitively constricted and narrow minded view of things. I just want to make an important point here. Don't worry; this isn't a "Yes Captain, I'm Awake" check.

Remember what Allport concluded in his book titled "The Nature of Prejudice"? Fortunately, Allport understood that human beings entered the world with tolerant attitudes. Allport asserted:

> *"Human nature seems, on the whole, to prefer the sight of kindness and friendliness to the sight of cruelty...Normal men everywhere...like to live in peace and friendship with their neighbors; they prefer to love and be loved than to hate and be hated."*

The formation of a tolerant or intolerant attitude depends upon whether our parents expressed love, acceptance, consistent discipline, and how well they provided us with a moral foundation and guidance. Our parents are responsible for explaining and demonstrating how to accept cultural differences in other children. Children who received this kind of training were more likely to become caring, open-minded, and compassionate adults. If children didn't receive this kind of training, they tended to become fearful, insecure, distrustful, anxious, and self-centered.

Stereotyping

How familiar are you with the term ***stereotype***? I know you're familiar with the word. But do you know its true definition? Remember the "Us and Them" thinking? Well the "Us and Them" thinking can lead to stereotypes. A stereotype is a distorted image or perception someone has of some member of a group. So, if you're in the "Us" group, then I'm in the "Them" group. Since I'm in the "Them" group, you decide what elements of my behavior place me and my friends in the "Them" group. The aspects of my behavior that placed me in the "Them" group may or may not be related to my being Jewish. For example, some people stereotype Jews as thrifty and controlling. Now, there may be some Jews who are thrifty, just like some Christians and Buddhists are thrifty. So, sometimes there may be an element of truth in stereotypes. In other words, there are probably some Jews who are thrifty, but I suspect that the majority of Jews are not thrifty.

Stereotypes can be difficult to remove. For starters, human beings tend to remember the undesirable or negative behaviors of others. We also remember past behaviors that confirm our stereotypes of certain individuals in culture groups. Finally, if we have insufficient information about other people's behavior, we tend to fabricate material consistent with the stereotype to fill in the gaps of information. Behavioral and social researchers have concluded that human beings stereotype because of cognitive limitations in processing information. It's just a self-serving sort of maneuver, you know, creating cognitive categories to deal with over stimulation. It's a strategy for making sense of our world. Ernest Becker wrote the following about stereotypes:

> *"But when one is dealing with massively unpredictable human objects, dependable cues for inference are not easy to come by. Therefore, man is given to stereotyping in the interests of his own security.*

If you think all Jews are thrifty, you are probably over generalizing. Contemporary research consistently demonstrates that Jews, in proportion to their numbers, give more generously to charities than other cultures in proportion to their numbers. So, if Jews are thrifty why would they be so generous and charitable? In Judaism, there is a practice known as ***Tzedaka*** that is taught to Jewish children. Tzedaka means performing deeds of justice or donating money so that acts of kindness can be performed for the less fortunate. As a child, I attended Arie Crown Hebrew Day School in Chicago. Arie Crown was an Orthodox Hebrew Day School. As a child in Hebrew School, I was taught that Tzedaka was one of the most important obligations a Jew could fulfill. My kids gave Tzedaka when they went to Hebrew School.

Let's finish with stereotypes. The problem with stereotypes is that the person doing the stereotyping believes that all members of the group being stereotyped behave similarly or share common characteristics. Although most stereotypes are negative perceptions of others, some may be positive. After stereotypes are created, they tend to persist even when the person holding the stereotype is presented with contradictory evidence. It's about what has to happen for someone to give up the cultural assumption they have about someone. An individual holding a stereotype will keep it because it serves some useful purpose in his/her life. Okay, he/she may take $10 and a pint of Ben and Jerry's to give it up. Otherwise, he/she will not give it up because it'll create too much anxiety and discomfort. I know that we create stereotypes because our brain looks for efficient ways to process new information and organize and categorize experiences. Stereotypes are comforting because they allow us to kind of predict how people will behave in a world full of unpredictability.

Selective Perception

Stereotypes also result in ***selective perception*** where the person holding the stereotype tends to see only what fits the stereotype and to ignore other perceptions that don't fit. Why do you think people do this? Do you think it's because people want to be right when it comes to perceiving and predicting how others will behave? In other words, they want to see the person they are observing behave in ways that are consistent with their stereotypes of that person. If you think Jews are thrifty, controlling, and can't be trusted, then you will subconsciously look for them to behave this way.

Social Constructionism

Yes, *social constructionism.* It's another one of those fancy and expensive words. You paid a lot of money for this book, so naturally it will contain some fancy, expensive words. I mean, I've got an assumption you'll pretty much value what I am saying a hole lot more if I use enough fancy words. Social constructionism means there are no universal truths about human beings and nature because human beings construct reality based on their culture. Remember, cultures aren't the same. It keeps coming back to what works for me won't necessarily work for you. If all cultures were the same, we'd have universal truths and moral absolutes. We could probably agree on some *moral absolutes,* such as all cultures should prevent their members from dying of malnutrition and from being physically abused. All cultures should also treat life as sacred. These are examples of moral absolutes. I know, up above I wrote, "hole" instead of "whole." I know I did that. Did you catch this "Yes Captain, I'm awake" check?

7

"All right, What Am I Supposed to Do Now?"

○ ○

"Cruelty can arise from the aesthetic outrage we sometimes feel in the presence of strange individuals who seem to be making out all right…Have they found some secret passage to eternal life? It can't be. If those weird individuals with beards and funny hats are acceptable, then what about my claim to superiority? Can someone like that be my equal in God's eyes? Does he, that one, dare hope to live forever too—and perhaps crowd me out? I don't like it. All I know is, if he's right I'm wrong. So different and funny looking. I think he's trying to fool the Gods with his sly ways. Let's show him up. He's not very strong. For a start, see what he'll do when I poke him."

—Alan Harrington

Now what? We've pretty much thrown a wide net over the field of cultural diversity, tolerance, culture bound values, socialization, and how you can be more culturally aware. We threw a smaller net over enrichment, social inequality, science, and religion. I know, our net caught lots of other social issues. I also asked you to think about why you purchased this book. Yes, I asked you lots of questions. How many of them have you answered? Don't just do it for me; you'd be patronizing me again. The desire to answer the difficult questions needs to come from deep inside of you, what we call intrinsic motivation as opposed to my insistence that you do it. You like that metaphor of the net? I like it very much.

I can't remember what else we discussed. Do you remember? Don't worry, this isn't a "Yes Captain, I'm Awake" check. Look, everything we discussed was related to you, me and them. How's that for a summary of what we discussed? Oh sure, I could have written more about what a vector inspector's typical day on the job was like or about different topical ointments. I could have derailed us more and written about my favorite existential writers, Kafka and Camus. But this isn't a book on existentialism. And don't brag and say you knew most of what I wrote about. Maybe a little of it. Just admit I taught you something, because the more you admit I did, the easier it'll be convincing yourself this book was worth $13.00 You don't want to relapse and develop "Post Purchase Cognitive Dissonance" again.

You know something, there are a lot of people who never get the "what you need to know" enrichment experience because of their resistance to knowing. Learning new things means integrating what you learned into your habitual ways of thinking and feeling. What you learn may lead you to seriously consider altering your value system. Altering your value system isn't easy. It's easier to change your attitude about something.

Some people deny they need to learn anything because their world is not confusing, unpredictable, or complicated. These people have an overly simplified perception of how society functions. Finally, some people know everything there is to know, like me. I've got a great fund of knowledge and had a lot of enrichment experiences. So, if you're tired of others haranguing you to enjoy an enrichment experience, just memorize what Rollo May said about Dostoevsky, who expressed this attitude very nicely:

> *"I think Dostoevsky was right, that every human being must have a point at which he stands against the culture, where he says, this is me and the damned world can go to hell"*

You know, sometimes a human being needs to be brave and insist that society do all the changing. A human being can tolerate only so much pressure to change. Period. Ever really reflect on what change means and why it's so difficult to do? There are individuals who are anxious and fearful of change because they may fail. For some people, change means modifying how they live their lives. Now, have you ever tried to modify how you live your life; you know, improve certain areas of your life? It's not easy. It's a lot easier to avoid changing because it reduces anxiety, fear and, I suppose, it's reinforcing to avoid situations that remind you to change. Know what I mean? You just avoid people, places and things that remind you of the need to change. It's like you'd become agoraphobic if all the changing you needed to do was out in the social world.

Goal Setting Behavior

What some people discover is that they fall short of the goals they set for themselves. I think falling short of something means you didn't make a serious enough commitment to achieve your goal. In other words, you didn't do the necessary things to achieve the goal. It wasn't important enough to change. Knowing your rationale to change isn't always enough. There's lots of things I know I need to change about myself, and I can articulate why I need to change, but I can't share with you right now, or probably later, what I need to change.

I'm not going to make a high-level self-disclosure here. It's about holding yourself, not me, your alter ego or a mysterious social force responsible for falling short of your desired goal. You may not know this brilliant aphorism about human behavior: *Human beings dislike responsibility.* Responsibility means setting and achieving higher standards for yourself. It means you're willing to ask more of yourself. It's about facing yourself in the mirror (a clean mirror so you look good when you look at it) and saying to yourself, "I'm going to get fit by walking three days a week. I'll get up before work, walk a half hour, and suck up as much of the sun and its energy as I can before I shower, eat a healthy breakfast and gear up for work." Period. Go ahead and reward yourself with a gourmet cup of coffee at your favorite coffee place and enjoy it on your ride to work. If you really need the extra pump, listen to Neil Young's "Like a Hurricane" or "Rockin' in the Free World" on your way to work. Both of these pieces are electric guitar. If you want something softer to transition to work, listen to his "Heart of Gold" or "Harvest Moon." Look, listening to Neil Young generates the mood I'm searching for at 5:30 in the morning when I'm training. It may not generate the mood you need to be in at 5:30 in the morning. It's just a suggestion. Thanks for listening.

Responsible Behavior

Responsibility and accountability. Break down the word responsibility and you get "response" and "ability." So, the question is: "Am I able to respond to this challenge I've set for myself?" Am I able? I am able! I am able-minded. I know what you're asking yourself right now. What's this got to do with cultural diversity? Absolutely nothing…well, yes it does. Responsible people set goals. I was trying to demonstrate that you wouldn't change unless you're committed to seriously changing. That's the connection. I know, only if you need changing in life. Remember this aphorism: Life is work. Life is the steadiest work you'll ever have.

You must act on life. Life doesn't act on you. Your alter ego doesn't act on you. I don't act on you. A lousy breakfast burrito can act on your stomach occasionally. That's pretty much it for who acts on whom for now. Here's a fancier way of saying you act on your life: "You are a self-directed, self-determined organism directing yourself in your environment of choice and controlling the social forces that affect your life." Okay, I'll soften it up and say that you control most of the conditions that affect your life. How's that? I'm not going to restate it anymore.

Ignorance, Substance, Depth and Profundity

You know, it's a lot easier to be ignorant. I know you know what I mean here. No one wants other people advising them to have a "what-you-need-to-know" experience. It's like what you and I experienced together, as opposed to you experiencing it alone, beginning with Chapter 1 where I insisted you needed a "what-you-need-to-know" enrichment experience. You know this idea of needing to know things reminds me of a quote by one of my favorite writers, Ernest Hemingway:

> *"Nobody knows what's in him until he tries to pull it out. If there's nothing, or very little, the shock can kill a man."*

I like this quote because it illustrates what can occur when we discover there's little substance or depth to our lives. Imagine someone not ever discovering there's little substance or depth to his or her life. It's simply a diverse world with people having varying degrees of substance and depth to them. I like it that way. Now, if this individual never has to pull anything out of him/herself, he'd never die of shock.

The other thing is that substance and depth are subjectively defined and relative. Substance and depth probably means different things to different people. For some people, it could simply mean that I'm pretty much all flesh and bones, with a few critical organs that enable me to continue inhaling, exhaling and evaluating things. A simple, functional and utilitarian life is what I like. That's it. Again, there's nothing wrong with this way of living. Other people see more than the flesh, bones and realization that they are alive and able to look things over more deeply. These people aren't any better than the functional, utilitarian people. It's just that they look to draw more out of life, challenging themselves to learn, to satisfy their curiosity instinct about why and how things occur in the world. This attitude, though, means investing time to follow through on things. Following through on things is synonymous with responsibility. Personal responsibility means holding yourself accountable to pursue the experience that will give your life substance and depth. Again, I'm not insisting everyone needs to add substance and depth to their lives. And don't be thinking that I need to add lots of substance and depth to my life. I wrote this book.

The Cultural Awareness Starter Kit

What are you going to do now that you have the cultural awareness starter kit? You worked through your "Button Resistant Disorder" and pushed the launch button. I'm glad you didn't sit on the launch pad for 32 years. We've covered a lot between the covers. I'm talking about the covers of this book. I provided you with an overview of cultural diversity and strategies for how you can modify your counterproductive stereotypes and biases about other cultures. For most people biases or stereotypes can be counterproductive. If I'm referring to you, keep seeking firsthand experiences with people from other cultures and learn the subtleties of their life ways.

Finally, check your cultural assumptions against what you're seeing while interacting with people. You might discover that your unfavorable cultural assumptions are inaccurate, and that only one or two individuals in the culture may behave in ways that substantiate your negative cultural assumptions. Remember, there's about two-percent truth in a stereotype. Philosophically speaking (as opposed to regularly speaking) being open to experiencing other cultures leaves you less lonely and alienated. The categorizing that results from stereotyping is real and potentially destructive. At this time in the world we need to interact with others in genuine, bias-free ways and together strive for cultural harmony.

As a culturally aware individual, you now know you must respect the individuality of people from other cultures. People from other cultures experienced a different socialization or cultural program than you, and have their own, unique life orientation to the world guided by a different language, and they have culture bound values just as valid as yours. A *life orientation* is a theory, a reliable one, about how you look at and interact with your world to satisfy your needs. Does that make sense? One way to understand that others have **multiple identities** is to admit that you are a diverse human being, an individual with your own multiple identities. These identities include being a father or mother, spouse, male or female, athlete or non-athlete, brother or sister, son or daughter, Republican or Democrat, butcher, lawyer or vector inspector. Seeing yourself as a diverse human being with multiple identities will help you experience others as diverse human beings, who are not given to simply being classified into arbitrary categories based on culture or race.

Reflecting on Things

Ever seriously reflect on things? In this instance, reflecting on things means thinking about your earliest memory of an experience with an individual from a culture other than your own. I hope you can retrieve one of those early memories. What do you remember about your first encounter with someone of a different culture or race? Think about it. You can also reflect on which individuals in your life have most influenced your attitudes about other races and cultures. I think you'll agree that your parents were responsible for inculcating your bias-free attitudes about other cultures. If you've done enough reflecting and now realize that you need to modify your attitudes about other cultures, go ahead and write an action plan.

An Action Plan

The first step of the **action plan** is being aware that other cultures exist. You can probably skip this step because you're pretty mature and observant. The second step is acknowledging that cultures can be complex and difficult to understand. Try not to generalize about individuals in a certain culture. The third step is to admit to yourself the validity of cultural differences. In other words, it's all right for other cultures to talk, behave and worship differently than you. It's a valid way of life and it's no better or worse than your way of life. By now, you should be more than aware, more conscious, that your culture, as wonderful as it is, isn't any better or worse than any other culture. You need to acknowledge that differences between cultures are not inherently negative. It's not that the culture-bound values of other cultures are bad, but that values, norms and customs are relative to a culture and can only be understood in terms of the survival function they serve in that culture. Finally, seeing individuals from other cultures in more positive and favorable ways doesn't mean you see yourself more negatively.

As part of your *action plan*, you need to also recognize that diversity exists everywhere and that it's unavoidable. It really is. Just look around you and you'll see diversity. I mean, you should see diversity. Do you? It applies to the physical world and, well, probably less so to the human world. What do you think? Which world does it apply more to? What about the animal world? As you can see, diversity is ever present, omnipresent and ubiquitous. I know, ever present, omnipresent and ubiquitous are synonymous. I just wanted to reinforce the assertion that diversity is, well, everywhere. The only time it isn't is if you're not inhaling, exhaling, and evaluating things.

Social Identity

You also need to feel secure and confident in your *social identity*. I'm not asking you to change your value system by exposing yourself to different cultures. You need to honor your life way and interact respectfully with other cultures. If you don't feel secure with your social identity, then you'll feel threatened experiencing other cultures. In other words, you'll be on shaky ground while exploring other life ways because what you see may cause you to question your own value system. Some people may simply refuse to learn about other cultures because they are too stuck in their own impenetrable cultural vault with their rigid, habitual ways of thinking. The reason I wrote vault is because it's awful difficult to break out of a vault. I know, good dynamite will bust you out.

A Fable About Institutionalizing Truth

I once heard this fable about truth and I liked it a lot. It illustrates what we're discussing here.

A man set out to climb to the top of a pretty high mountain. Satan learned he was hiking up the mountain and began to worry that the man might discover ultimate truth at the mountaintop. Maybe G-d would reveal things to him to bring back to the village. After thinking about this situation more, Satan concluded there was no need to worry. Satan realized that the man would encounter bigger problems after returning to the village. The man would have to institutionalize the truth.

Imagine having to institutionalize truth. It's tantamount to convincing everyone in America that the one and only true religion is Zoroastrianism. That's one example of trying to institutionalize truth. You could easily sustain some kind of injury institutionalizing any kind of truth if you're not careful. Especially if you get really passionate about it.

Since we're discussing cultures, I'll derail us by listing some basic human needs that are cultural universals, you know, things that most human beings need: love and intimacy, which includes sex; food, clothing and shelter; spirituality/religion; safety and health. What do you think of this list? Am I missing anything? Should I remove something? I know, people can be atheists and not need spirituality or religion. But they can get help for this problem. Just kidding.

A Little More on Culture-Bound Values

Let me remind you of the **culture bound values** of some North American individuals. Remember, I said some, which means a percentage of the population in America. You can decide what percentage of the population honors these values. We value our independence, autonomy, and believe in rugged individualism. The thinking is that a human being can control his or her environment. Individuals in this culture and society like to win. Another way to express this understanding is that we don't like losing. In this culture, time is money, it's divided into chunks and it's for this reason we adhere to fixed and rigid time schedules. Time is divided into chunks for economic use. We believe that hard work results in success. Most people plan for the future. We use a linear conceptualization to describe the life cycle and life cycle events. There is an over-reliance on science to understand our world, meaning we're trying to discover cause-and-effect relationships to explain how and when social and physical events occur. Christianity is usually the practiced faith. In this society, credentials, titles and owning expensive, fancy items are usually glamorized. What do you think?

How Cultures That Need to be Right Can be Dangerous

Since we're discussing culture here, I think we need to remember that war, racism and persecution have historically resulted because some cultures needed to be right about things. Think about it. Now that you've thought about it, do you agree? It's all right if you disagree, because I won't know if you disagree. If I knew you disagreed, then it wouldn't be all right for you to disagree. Just kidding. It's all right if you disagree with me because I'm tolerant and respectful of other opinions. The things that may incite war or tension between countries are conflicts over who the one, right G-d or race is or serious disagreements about the life styles of other cultures. As you can see, the tendency for a culture to dichotomize things into right and wrong can have very destructive consequences.

Typically, the dominant culture identifies itself as "Us" and it assigns the other culture the title of "Them." Once this label is applied, the differences between the two cultures create distance and tension. Cultures, like human beings, like to polarize things into right and wrong. The "Us" culture probably experiences the "Them" culture as threatening and too complicated to understand. So, because the "Them" culture threatens the "Us" culture, we have problems. If the "Us" culture didn't feel threatened by what it observed in the "Them" culture, then there wouldn't be as many problems. However, the differences between the two cultures are used by the "Us" culture to defend itself against becoming like the "Them" culture. In the end, the life ways of the "Them" culture threatens members of the "Us" culture by compelling them to examine their own cultural beliefs, values and what they define as truth.

As a people, we need to stop thinking that some cultures are more personally or religiously superior than others. All cultures contribute to the wonderful diversity of the world and where they are located in the world will influence their economic, artistic, religious, political, social and industrial development. As a people we must understand that we can enrich our lives by studying and gaining firsthand experiences of other cultures, and that by doing so we can discover new possible solutions to problems. I suppose, in the end, some cultures, by indoctrinating intolerant attitudes in their members, reinforce the belief that they are living right. Remember, intolerance reinforces conformity and a special group identity.

The Culture of Self-Importance

I now want to discuss a cultural phenomenon that concerns me. Just because it concerns me doesn't mean it needs to concern you. I never asserted that you needed to agree with me. Rather, I encouraged you to think critically about the material after I presented it to you in an objective, balanced way. I did, however, insist that you search for unbiased evidence so you can look at issues clearly. We discussed this in Chapter 1. For some of us, and again I'm not necessarily referring to you, there's a big infatuation with the self. This preoccupation with the self is pretty common around here. There are too many ordinary Hanks here and I've got to show everybody I'm no ordinary Hank. I'm a member of this privileged class that's doing all kinds of very important things. "Right now, I'm flying to this very high-level conference in Washington D.C. and then I'm going to a $1,000 a-plate fundraising dinner with important people. I can't talk to you now." These types of people are in love with themselves, their Porsches, yachts, and mansions on the bluff.

What do you think? Preoccupation with the *self* means feeling self-important, yearning for unlimited success and power, and needing very special treatment and constant admiration. Sometimes, it's exaggerating what one has achieved to gain more attention. I'll try not to exaggerate my achievements. I mean, I have lots of achievements, but I'm uncomfortable bragging about them. I'm all right with being perceived as an ordinary Hank doing lots of good in my circle of influence. Inside my circle are my mentally ill and older adult students, my friends and family. And yes, I've got lots of friends.

Some people—and this doesn't include me—have to exaggerate their accomplishments to distance themselves from the nearest privileged individual. Just get a gold-plated snake. You know, that device plumbers use to remove tree roots from your clogged pipes. In other words, don't spend too much time looking at him. Look at my gold-plated snake and me.

Inhale, Exhale and Look Around

I'm not sure now why I'm discussing preoccupation with the self. Maybe it's because being in love with yourself diminishes your desire to reach out to others; to make others feel important, worthwhile, to affirm their right to be treated with dignity and to make meaningful contributions. Yes, that's the connection to intercultural communication. We need to notice individuals from other cultures and not be overly aware of ourselves. You're pretty much already aware of yourself, aren't you? I think that by now, you've got a very sophisticated explanation for how you know you're alive. Inhale, exhale and look around. A lot of people look around but forget to inhale and exhale. And there are some people who inhale, exhale and don't look around at all. I suppose there are lots of things we can do with inhaling, exhaling and looking around. Some people inhale, exhale and don't do anything with what they see. Others inhale, exhale, look around and act on things they see. I think the pluralist attitude is the ideal perspective on things. Here, the individual inhales, exhales, looks around and concludes that all of the people around have legitimate life ways that can teach them things about his or her life and world. How do you like that? It's a very nice approach to life.

The Exclusivist, Inclusivist and Pluralist Views on Things

Here are a few perspectives to consider when thinking about other cultures. Think about which view is closest to yours. The *exclusivist* asserts that his/her culture is the only right way to live. The *inclusivist* proclaims that his/her culture is right for him/her and he/she can understand how your culture is right for you. The *pluralist* affirms that all cultures are legitimate ways of living and have a potential to teach all of us important things. Which view did you select? I'll respect your view. If you're an exclusivist, I'll respect your view. If you're an inclusivist or a pluralist, I'll give you a $1.00 rebate on my book. And don't just say you're an inclusivist or pluralist. Remember, our relationship is based on trust, even when money is involved.

Self-Reflecting

I've been reminding you throughout this book to self-reflect. If you do enough self-reflecting, like dedicating about six hours a day to self-reflect, you'll be one sharp self-reflector. Okay, how about 10 to 15 minutes for each session of self-reflecting, three days a week? If you've got good self-reflection, then you have a good, deep understanding of yourself and your interpersonal behavior. It means you can analyze why you behave certain ways around others. I suppose it means you're in touch with yourself; you know what's going on inside of you. Other people in our culture are actually very good at advising us what's going on inside of us. That's been occurring in our culture for a good long time now.

I'm delighted that you chose to spend $13.00 on this book. You could have bought other things for about the same price, like a highly discounted T-shirt with a logo, three pairs of socks, a couple of meals or a 10-pack of self-stick removable notes. So, thanks a lot for purchasing the book. In all honesty, as compared to me being partially honest with you, I very much appreciate you supporting my work. Again, I'm just trying to sustain job stability as a writer. I hope you have job stability. I want you to have lots of successful launches in your life. Be sure that your launch kit includes all the tools you'll need to make your landing a great one. Don't put an anvil in your launch kit. It'll just weigh you down. You don't want to fall short of your launch destination now. Remember, use your one and only life to do what William James advised us to do with it:

"The best use of a life is to spend it for something that will outlast it"

I like this quote a whole lot. James is suggesting that we use our life to counsel others about how to make it in the world. Assist others whenever possible. Be an everyday hero. An everyday hero does good in the world; performing acts of care. A heroic act performed by an everyday hero fulfills a moral objective and influences the lives of others. An everyday hero leaves a legacy for the world and the people he or she has helped. We need to be virtuous; to trust that every act of kindness performed gets written in the celestial archive; that we're here to add to our life and the life of others; and that life can, of course, be tricky and unforgiving at times.

The End

I need to bring this chapter to its natural end. Natural because ending things any other way would be unnatural. Ending things in a natural way means it's supposed to end now as opposed to ending later. So, now is the time to end the book. Thanks again so much for believing that together, we can make a difference in the world by challenging ourselves to being more open and accepting of individuals from other cultures. I admire your courage for exploring your biases and seeking freedom from the bondage of distorted perceptions of others. No more dichotomous, habitual ways of thinking and interacting with others. It's so liberating to experience others fully and genuinely, in unbiased ways free of how others want you to think about people. It's just too limiting. I cannot falsely construct the self I show the world through you; by asserting I know who I am, what I'm about, simply because I am not you.

In the end, my culture and religion is not more right or true than yours. I am not personally and culturally superior to you. I am not a better human being than you. G-d won't look on me more favorably because I'm on his side with my faith. We need to honestly ask ourselves this question: What is one of your noblest aspirations in life? If it is to allow people who are culturally different to belong to, be treated with dignity and to contribute to your world, then you're a great human being.

Finally, human beings are too complex to be categorized. I mean, you can't just put me in that cubbyhole and expect me to eat plain brown M &Ms for the rest of my life. I like the plain red M&Ms and the green peanut M&Ms, too. I'm a pluralist. Thanks a whole lot now. I really mean it.

Bibliography

Allport, Gordon W. (1954/1979) *The nature of prejudice.* Reading, MA: Addison-Wesley.

Becker, Ernest (1971) *The birth and death of meaning.* (2nd ed.) New York: Free Press.

Becker, Ernest (1973) *The denial of death.* New York: Free Press.

Durkheim, Emile (1954) *The elementary forms of the religious life.* New York: Free Press.

Hodge, Robert, Treiman, D. and Rossi, Peter ((1966) *Class, status and power.* (2nd ed.) New York: Free Press

Maslow, Abraham H. (1962) *Toward a psychology of being.* (1st edition) Princeton, NJ: Van Nostrand

Whorf, Benjamin (1956) *Language, thought and reality.* New York: Wiley

0-595-31361-2